A Joyful Pilgrimage

MY LIFE IN COMMUNITY

Emmy Arnold

PLOUGH PUBLISHING HOUSE

Published by Plough Publishing House
Walden, New York
Robertsbridge, England
Elsmore, Australia
www.plough.com

© 1999 by Plough Publishing House
All Rights Reserved.

The photographs in this book are from the
Bruderhof Historical Archive.

This book was originally published in 1964
as *Torches Together*, with reprints in 1971 and 1976.

ISBN (10-digit): 0-87486-956-0
ISBN (13-digit): 978-0-87486-956-9

A catalog record for this book is available from the British Library.
Library of Congress Cataloging-in-Publication Data
Arnold, Emmy.
   A joyful pilgrimage : my life in community / Emmy Arnold.
      p. cm.
   Rev. ed. of : Torches together.
   ISBN 0-87486-956-0 (pbk.)
   1. Bruderhof Foundation--History.   2. Arnold, Eberhard, 1883–1935.
3. Arnold, Emmy.   I. Arnold, Emmy. Torches together. II. Title.
Bx8129.B64A8 1999
289.7'092--dc21
   [b]
                                                         99-45951
                                                             CIP

Contents

Editor's Note

It was natural that as the only founder of the Bruderhof still alive after World War II, Emmy Arnold would one day be asked to tell her story. She was already in her seventies when she began the project, but the details she recounted were as alive for her as if they had happened the day before.

The original, handwritten German manuscript for *A Joyful Pilgrimage* evolved from the author's notes, some made as early as the 1930s. By the 1960s there were several bound volumes of these. "I don't want these events and people to be forgotten," she would say. In 1964, a book-length manuscript was prepared, translated, and published as *Torches Together*.

For this new edition, aside from making revisions and factual corrections, new details and anecdotes have been incorporated. Though some are the result of recent research, most of them come from an unpublished diary of the author's, *Das Geschlossene Buch,* and from other personal papers.

As a book that records both the trials and joys of living a new way in a new era, it is fitting that this new edition of Emmy Arnold's memoirs can be made available to a wider readership. For it was never nostalgia or a sentimental yearning for old times that animated her. Rather, she was driven forward by her vision of a future society built on justice and love, and by her expectant longing for the coming of the kingdom.

1

Origins

As I was asked to write down the story of my life, I want to tell a little of everything I remember. I especially want to tell about the first years of the Bruderhof communities (since I am one of the few who still remember them) and how we were visited and moved by the Spirit in spite of our human weakness and failings. I don't really know where to begin, but because my personal background somehow belongs to it all, I will start there.

My husband, Eberhard, and I both stem from upper-middle-class academic circles. Both of us enjoyed protected childhoods, and we were rather isolated from people of other classes. Although both of us always felt we owed a great debt of gratitude to our parents, we also felt we must go our own ways. Somehow we did not feel that our lives were complete. We longed for a fuller, more meaningful life and could not help feeling a certain boredom.

Eberhard was born on July 26, 1883, in Königsberg, East Prussia. His father, Carl Franklin Arnold (born in Williamsfield, Ohio, on March 10, 1853), taught in the grammar school at Königsberg at the time Eberhard was born. Eberhard's mother, Elisabeth Arnold (formerly Voigt), came from traditional academic circles. She was born on September 20, 1852, in Oldenburg, Germany. Eberhard was the third child in the family. He had one brother and three sisters. When he was still a young boy his father became Professor of Theology and Church History at the University of Breslau in Silesia.

I have been told that in his boyhood days Eberhard was very lively—full of mischief—and that he caused quite a lot of trouble, especially for his teachers. They, as well as the parents of his school-mates, were not always pleased with the influence he had on the other students. Already at that time he felt drawn to poor people and

Eberhard Arnold at fourteen.

tramps. He found these people much more natural and warm-hearted than those of the middle class. This was hard for his parents to understand, and a number of conflicts resulted. Once, for instance, Eberhard befriended a passing tramp; by the end of the encounter, they had traded hats, and soon afterward his mother discovered lice!

At sixteen, Eberhard was no longer satisfied with the stuffiness of life at home. That summer he spent his vacation at the rectory of an uncle, Ernst Ferdinand Klein, at Lichtenrade near Berlin. There he was exposed to a kind of Christianity he had never known before.

Through a personal experience of Christ at his former parish in Silesia, where there were many badly underpaid weavers, Onkel Ernst had decided to support the poor. This had brought him a good deal of hostility from wealthier parishioners, and he had been forced to give up his pastorate.

Once Eberhard was present during a talk his uncle had with a young officer of the Salvation Army. He followed what was said with eager interest. The brotherly way in which these two men conversed, and the love of Christ which he saw in both, aroused in the sixteen-year-old a deep longing to find the source of this love for himself.

On returning home from this vacation, Eberhard began to seek more earnestly to find Christ. Later he told me how in October of 1899, after a prolonged inner struggle, he had visited a young pastor one day after hearing him speak. When he asked the pastor about the Holy Spirit, the pastor said, "It is just this Spirit that has led you here." So it happened that Eberhard experienced conversion.

Eberhard was very moved when he told me about this time in his life. It was the same period when the Fellowship Movement (which started in England and America) was spreading in Germany,

Switzerland, and other countries as well. Members of this movement felt Christ was more than the Son of God: he was their Redeemer. But it went beyond that. People met in private homes, forming groups and fellowships in which they worshiped together. Something had begun to move. Immediately after his own conversion, Eberhard tried to establish contact with these groups.

As a first step he talked with his parents and teachers in an effort to straighten things out. Alas, they neither understood nor believed him. One teacher even thought Eberhard was playing a joke and sent him out of the room as a prankster! But step by step people began to accept the fact that he was indeed earnest. Classmates soon gathered around him and a small group came into being. As a result, Eberhard's room was hardly ever empty, and he had great difficulty applying himself to his schoolwork.

The situation became worse when Eberhard began to associate with the Salvation Army. Drawn by its attempts to put Christianity into action, and by its concern for the plight of the downtrodden, he frequently attended its meetings. He also visited, with its members, some of the worst sections of Breslau at night. Eberhard did this, he later told me, because he felt called to save those who were lost and to reach out to the most desperate people of the "submerged tenth," as old Salvation Army General William Booth used to call them.

Naturally this development caused a great deal of excitement at home, especially when Eberhard's parents read large posters all over town saying, "Attention! Salvation Army. Tonight missionary Eberhard Arnold will address a large meeting." Grammar school boys were legally prohibited to engage in public speaking, and Eberhard's disregard for the law did nothing but aggravate his already strained relationship with his parents. Already then (as several times later) Eberhard's father feared that he would be forced to give up his professorship at the university because of this ill-mannered son who was destroying his good name.

Soon school authorities put an end to Eberhard's public appearances, and his parents, making use of an opportunity to change his environment, sent him to the little town of Jauer for further studies. At Jauer, Eberhard was supposed to prepare for his final exams, undisturbed by all these interruptions. Yet even there a small group gathered around him for regular Bible study. All the same, Eberhard was able to graduate. Many years later, even after his death, I met people who had not forgotten this time of Eberhard's youth—so great was his zeal for Jesus. Many said they received an inner direction for their entire life during those days.

For a while Eberhard wondered whether he should join the Salvation Army. During one summer, while vacationing at the North Sea, he wrestled with this question as never before. His love for those who were "lost" and unjustly treated—those for whom Christ had come—drew him toward the Salvation Army. Yet he realized more and more that they approached things in a rather one-sided, religious way, and that they lacked a certain depth in the way they handled the various social problems with which they were confronted.

Eberhard decided, then, not to join the Salvation Army, though he always maintained a special feeling of friendship and love for its members. Right to the end of his life he continued to attend their meetings when he could, and even to speak at them on occasion.

Now I want to tell about my own childhood and youth. I was born on December 25, 1884, in Riga, Latvia, as the second child of Heinrich and Monika (formerly Otto) von Hollander. There were five girls and two boys in our family. I remember very little of my early childhood because I was only five years old when we left our homeland. The Russian presence was growing steadily in the city, and like many other German-Baltic families, we immigrated to Germany to escape this influence; our parents wanted us to be brought up as Germans. I never saw Riga again. We left to settle in Jena in the spring of 1890.

I don't know whether it was because I was born on December 25th, but Christmas—the time when the Christ Child was born for the salvation of humankind—was always something heavenly for me. As I grew older, the meaning of this special holiday touched me to the depths of my heart and influenced me strongly.

My best playmate and lifelong comrade was my sister Else, only eleven-and-a-half months younger than I, with whom I shared everything. Right until the end of her life we understood each other well.

Else (L) and Emmy (R) von Hollander in Riga, ca. 1890. Inseparable as children, they remained close until Else's death in 1932.

As children, we got into a lot of mischief together. I was always the leader, but Else joined in with enthusiasm.

They tell me that I was quite a wild little girl: there was no tree too high for me to climb, and no passing train that I wouldn't try to keep up with by running alongside it. I was too lively and wild for my mother's liking, and she often said, "You ought to have been a boy!" The more she said this, the more reserved I became toward her.

When I entered school in the spring of 1891, I had little interest in learning. My teacher was the strict Fräulein Ludewig, who was more interested in model pupils than in a tomboy like me. I could not sit still in school. I could hardly wait for recess or the end of class to get to my play and to thinking up new pranks. But in spite of all this wildness and naughtiness something different—perhaps it was an urge to find God—began to grow within me. When my little brother died suddenly at the age of nine months, I pondered where he and others who had died had gone, and when I looked up at the stars I wondered if he was on one of them.

After moving to Germany, my father repeated his examinations in order to be certified as a doctor of law; he hoped to be accepted for a professorship at Jena University. Unfortunately this did not work out, so we moved to Weimar, where my father had received an offer from the Grand Duke of Sachsen-Weimar for the position of court lawyer.

Everything was elegant and stiff in the Sophienstift, the school I attended in Weimar. The aristocratic families kept to themselves, looking down on middle-class pupils and refusing to mix with them. They were really a caste to themselves. In general, my sisters and I associated with these girls—we were expected to—but we would have much rather run through the fields or played in the woods as we had in Jena.

We lived in Weimar for only one-and-a-half years, but during that time I experienced the deaths of several people I knew personally, and this made a lasting impression on me.

At the children's Sunday services I attended, the message of the gospel fell deeply into my heart. I promised myself even then not to live for myself, but for God and my neighbor. I was probably about eleven then. My mother in particular, but others as well, had little understanding for my "strangeness"—on the one hand, my moments of searching for religious truth, and on the other, my tendency to be unruly and carefree.

As young girls, Lisa Franke (L) and Emmy (R) decided to devote their lives to serving God among the poor and sick.

My father was not happy with his position for long. After spending the summer of 1897 in Bad Berka, we moved to Halle on the Saale in October. At first I was among the troublemakers, but through my friendship with a girl my age, Lisa Franke, I experienced a renewed longing for God and Christ. I never spoke about this to anyone but Lisa—I was only thirteen—

but because she shared my childlike, living faith, we felt close to one another from the start. Two things drew me to Lisa: first, we both abhorred the flirting that went on among our classmates, and we would not even read love stories. Second, we were both intent on our search for a true Christian life. We agreed that we both wanted to remain celibate, become deaconesses, and serve the sick when we grew up: that was surely the best way to serve God and our neighbor.

Soon I began to go to church and to attend religious meetings on my own, and brought home books such as those by and about Zinzendorf, Otto Franke's *Footprints of the Living God on My Way of Life,* and Thomas à Kempis' *Imitation of Christ.* For several years Lisa and I attended the children's services held by Pastor Meinhof and Pastor Freybe. The latter's determination to lead a Christian life made a deep impression on me.

In 1901 my school days came to an end, and I began to take a more active part in Halle's church life. I read more, too, and was especially interested in the Moravian Count Zinzendorf (1700–1760) and the founding of Herrnhut, his Christian community.

A good friend from this time was Pastor Hans Busch, with whom I often visited the elderly and the sick of our parish. These were poor homes, and they smelled terrible; the conditions were sometimes so bad I could hardly enter them. But again and again I pulled myself together; I felt that love must overcome my emotions.

In the meantime, life at home became more difficult. My father was not happy in Halle, probably because he was not advancing in his career as he had hoped. I did not understand all the tensions.

At Easter 1902, when I was seventeen, I began working part-time at the Deaconess House. Because of my age, I was not allowed to sleep there, but had to live at home with my parents. In the beginning I worked only a few days a week, relieving other nurses, but soon I was granted a full-time job in the children's ward, where I saw a lot of suffering.

In 1903, when my youngest sister Margarethe, then fourteen, died in this ward as a result of appendicitis, I decided, again, that I had to find a deeper purpose for my life. I couldn't stand the thought of remaining at home with my sisters, just another daughter in another middle-class family. But after Margarethe's death, my parents asked me to return home; they wanted to have their five remaining children around them. Around this time the new head nurse at the Deaconess House was causing me problems at work, so I agreed to take a break, at least for a while.

The next May I went to live with the family of Pastor Freybe, who had lost their seven-year-old son and asked me to come and live with them. I will never forget those months at the parsonage. Discussions about how best to dedicate one's life to Christ characterized the whole of my stay there. I visited the sick and aged in the parish, took turns at the night watch, and cared for many little children. Shortly before Christmas I returned home.

At the age of twenty (in June 1905), I began working as a probationer nurse at the Halle Deaconess House, as I had now reached the required age. At first I worked in the women's wards. The shifts were long and the work hard; there were no eight-hour days. Life in the Deaconess House was very much like life in a convent. We had many religious services, and learned about the essence of life. "What do I want? I want to serve. Whom do I want to serve? The Lord in his poor and needy people. And if I grow old doing this? Then my heart will thrive like a palm tree. And if I die doing it? Queen Esther said, 'If I perish, I perish,' and she did not know Him for whose sake one can die."

All this gave me great joy. After several weeks, I was given the deaconess probationer's dress and cap, and there was a celebration for the newly uniformed assistant nurses. It was impressed upon us once more what a serious step it was to become a deaconess.

Unfortunately I became ill some time later. My father asked that I be given four weeks' leave, but this was refused: the pastor of the Deaconess House said that employees could be taken care of there, by fellow nurses. But my father was unyielding. What was I to do? I finally decided to go home.

In February 1906, after several weeks convalescing, I began work in the district hospital at Salzwedel, where I nursed men. Things were very different in Salzwedel from what they had been in the Deaconess House. There were religious rites, it is true, but little godliness. Instead, ambition and jealousy divided the nurses and made the work, which was already strenuous, even harder. Two of the young men I looked after died in a typhus epidemic; then Hertha, a close friend of mine in Halle who was just twenty years old, died of appendicitis. These deaths sobered me and challenged me to dedicate myself to something of significance — to live for what is eternal and imperishable.

In spring 1907 I went home for a vacation. What I was to experience there was

Emmy (R) and a fellow probationer playing bocce, 1906.

completely unexpected, as well as new and exciting. I had actually planned to stay home for only a few weeks of rest, as I felt called to the work I had chosen, but now my life really began.

At that time Ludwig von Gerdtell, a well-known public speaker, had just completed a series of lectures in the largest hall of Halle. His topics were "The atonement of Christ," "Can modern man still believe in the resurrection of Jesus?" "Is there sufficient historical evidence that Christ rose from the dead?" and others. Although I had not heard von Gerdtell myself, I was drawn to him through the enthusiastic accounts of my brother and sisters, through friends and acquaintances, and even through people in shops or on the street.

As the saying went, "all of Halle is standing on its head." People would approach complete strangers and ask them what they thought of these lectures. It was as if the whole town was breathing a new spirit, and I longed to be gripped by it too. Once I was able to get hold of von Gerdtell's lectures in print and read them, it wasn't long before I *was* a part of this movement, its call to repentance, and its search for radical inward change. With sharp words the call rang out: "Repent, for the kingdom of heaven is at hand!" I felt struck in my heart — judged — and began to set my personal life in order. More important, I began to seek contact with others who had been similarly moved.

People from all walks of life joined the revival, although in Halle it was mainly those who belonged to the "better" or "academic" circles. They would meet in private homes, for instance in the house of Frau Else Baehr, wife of the city's surgeon general, or of Frau Schulz, the wife of a leading ophthalmologist. These women opened their large drawing rooms for meetings, lectures, and discussions. People like Paul Zander (who later became a skilled surgeon) and his fiancée Lene Örtling, Karl Heim (later a famous professor at Tübingen), and Sigmund von Salwürk (a well-known artist and painter) had turned to Christ and were studying the life of the early Christians and their "primitive" faith together with others. No church, no sect, but an alliance of all believers!

On March 4, 1907, my sisters Else and Monika were invited to an evening meeting at Frau Baehr's house. A friend of Dr. von Gerdtell's, a theology student named Eberhard Arnold was to speak. Else and Moni (as we called Monika) had no special desire to go, whereas I was more interested. My parents were not in favor of my going into a strange private home. In those days this was not often done, unless one was at least somehow acquainted with the family. Strangely, though I was somewhat nervous about it, I felt drawn in every fiber of my being. So I went. Eberhard spoke on the Letter to the Hebrews, chapter ten: "Since we have confidence to enter the sanctuary by the blood of Jesus...let us draw near with a true heart in full assurance of faith."

After the meeting Eberhard was surrounded by people asking him about how these words could be put into practice. I held back, though I felt deeply challenged, and finally left for home. All the same I could not forget that evening: the love of Christ that spoke through Eberhard's words filled me so strongly, it was as if it were pursuing me. One day, still deeply moved by the experience, I went to Frau Baehr to try to tell her what had concerned me for so long. I was by nature very shy about revealing such personal things, but more than ever it seemed a matter of eternity, and of the call to life-long discipleship.

On the Sunday before Easter (March 24, 1907) Eberhard and I met again in the house of the ophthalmologist Schulz, where Bernhard Kühn was giving a talk. Kühn was a small, deformed man, but full of life and fire, and he penetrated the hearts of his listeners with his prophetic vision of God's future. "It does not yet appear what we shall be, but we know that when he appears we shall be like him, for we shall see him as he is" (1 John 3:2). All those present were deeply moved by this message. A few spoke and witnessed to what Christ meant to them for their future. Rather shyly, I also stood up for the first time and said that from now on my life would belong only to Christ.

I did not miss any of the next revival meetings, so deeply was I stirred by the truth and clarity of the gospel. After several of them Eberhard accompanied me home. From the start we understood each other in our common seeking, and we were both animated by the spirit that we felt was leading us. We talked about the meetings, about Jesus' guidance in our lives, and about our enthusiasm for a life given over to him alone. Some weeks later Eberhard told me that he had instinctively felt, from the first moment he saw me, that we belonged together.

When taking leave of me on the last evening of the series, on March 27, Eberhard asked me whether I felt, like he did, that God had led us together. I answered yes, and from that moment on felt myself bound to him. I told my parents that I felt as if I were engaged. The formal engagement took place on Good Friday, March 29, when Eberhard called on my parents to ask for their permission to marry me. At first they refused, but then they allowed us to talk together alone. We talked and prayed, read the thirty-fourth Psalm together, and gave our lives into the hands of God. We now considered ourselves engaged. My parents were ready to accept this, on the condition that Eberhard's parents also agreed.

From the outset, the time of our engagement was one of joy and enthusiasm, even as we sought and struggled. We wanted to give our lives to Christ, to save the lost, to comfort the downtrodden, and call sinners to repentance. We sought help and encouragement from friends and associates in the new groups already formed or in the process of formation. We read together from the Acts of the Apostles and from the letters of Paul, John, and Peter. We also tried to study the Revelation of John, but understood only a little of it.

During their almost three years of engagement, Eberhard and Emmy were together only rarely. Eberhard was away at the university; in addition, Emmy's parents imposed a six-month separation in the hope of discouraging the young couple from leaving the State church and accepting adult baptism.

Eberhard was able to come to Halle only for visits, as he was studying in Breslau for the semester. I did not return to Salzwedel, partly because I was overworked, but also because I could not tear myself away from the revival movement spreading through Halle.

Eberhard and I were eager to find unity with Christ and to establish a close relationship with those who were striving toward the same goal. We wanted to understand how the first Christians had lived, and what they believed. Through this the social question, and the question of what it truly means to be part of a church, became very acute for us. We realized to what an extent the life we knew was divided into classes and castes. Many people, including ourselves, enjoyed a position of privilege, not only in worldly possessions but also in an intellectual sense, and they had almost nothing in common with others less fortunate than themselves.

We tried to find clarity in all these things, and it was a special gift of our engagement time that we felt so united in our seeking.

The nine volumes of letters we exchanged while we were engaged (which I still have today) contain many of our insights, strivings, and agonizings.

Of the last there were plenty, for our parents on both sides were unable to understand our revolutionary approach to the problem of social justice and to the questions of baptism and the church. Regarding baptism, for example, it seemed obvious to us that the institutional church stood on a completely wrong foundation by receiving infants with birthright membership. We felt mature individuals should take this step voluntarily, on the basis of their own faith. When this became clear, a bitter struggle ensued with our families, and they used every possible means to try to prevent us from being baptized. (There is more about this in the book *Seeking for the Kingdom,* which includes selections from the letters written during the almost three years of our engagement.) Added to this difficulty was my parents' fear that I would influence and "infect" my brother and my sisters on the issue of baptism, as nearly all of them were already deeply involved in the revival movement.

The matter came to a head when Eberhard was disqualified from sitting for his doctoral examinations in theology because he was not willing to become a pastor in the state church. When my father and mother found out about this they were more upset than ever. "How can a man bind a woman to himself without having first established a sound economic basis for their future family?" In my parents' eyes, Eberhard's attitude was one of utter irresponsibility.

Not long afterward, at Erlangen, Eberhard switched courses and began preparing for doctoral examinations in philosophy. He was successful in passing these about a year later, at the end of November 1909. In spite of the many responsibilities he had at the time as a lecturer and student counselor, he passed with highest honors, *summa cum laude.* This by no means guaranteed a secure financial basis for our future, but we reminded my father of his promise: he could place no further obstacles in the way of our marrying once Eberhard received his Ph.D. My father hesitated at first, but finally he handed over my documents. Later the same day we went to the registrar and announced our intention to marry, a formality which had to be completed three weeks before the wedding. We chose the first date possible for this: December 20. At last the prolonged period of suspense and uncertainty would be over!

Since our engagement in the spring of 1907, I had never been in the same place for long. Aside from the conflict with my parents, various circumstances had made it impossible for me to stay at home, and I had lived in various towns across Germany, staying with friends or with families whose children I cared for. Friends nicknamed me "the flying Dutchman" after my maiden name, "von Hollander."

Luckily everything finally came to a good end, and the wedding took place in my parents' house, in a manner in keeping with our own convictions. Eberhard's parents and most of his brothers and sisters took part in the ceremony. Like the rest of the relatives, they had had initial objections, advising us to wait until we had a sound economic basis. We, however, wanted to found our common life entirely on faith. This faith never let us down.

2

Seeking

During the first few months of our married life Eberhard held many public meetings, often jointly with Ludwig von Gerdtell. At that time von Gerdtell was holding meetings in the largest hall in Leipzig, the city where we had our first home. He lived in our home for about six weeks in the early spring of 1910. This was not a very livable situation because of his insistence on a health-food diet, and because of other eccentricities.

Eberhard traveled a good deal, addressing crowds in public halls in Halle, Magdeburg, Dessau, Erfurt, Berlin, and other places. He was supported and financed by various groups that were part of the revival movement of that time. The lectures held at the Wintergarten in Halle, and in the Neumarkt clubhouse, were especially incisive and had far-reaching consequences. The first was attended by almost

Dr. Arnold:

Vortragssaal Spielgartenstr. 43

Montag, 4. Dezember: **Befreiung des Einzelnen.**

Dienstag, 5. Dezember: **Freiheit und Einheit.**

Eintritt frei!   Beginn 8½ Uhr.   *Eintritt frei!*

"The Freeing of the Individual" and "Freedom and Unity" – poster advertising a public lecture series in Magdeburg, 1911.

a thousand people. His topics included: "Jesus in opposition to the church," "The suffering and enslavement of the masses," "Jesus as he really was," "Following Christ," and "The future of God."

I accompanied my husband on his journeys as often as I could, and we experienced many an hour together when we felt the movement of God's spirit powerfully among us. People, old and young, would break down under the weight of their guilt and sin and turn eagerly toward a new life. At other times, we met with conflict. One time, for example, a professor stood up and urged the audience to leave the hall in protest: he was upset because Eberhard had "attacked" the institutional churches by saying they were built on a faulty foundation.

Often people came to visit our home for personal counseling, and the talks sometimes continued throughout the day. On many occasions I had to help when women came. The question arose frequently: how can we find a completely new way of life? In the most difficult situations we tried to offer our services by taking someone into our home.

In 1912 we experienced a terrible tragedy: after Eberhard had spoken at a public meeting, a stranger handed him a letter. In it the writer, a woman, asked him to come to her home that same evening, and went on to say, "If I had not been present at your meeting tonight, all of us–my husband, our children, and I–would not be alive tomorrow morning. This is our last hope." Eberhard hurried to the address written on the envelope and found the writer. She was a dressmaker, her husband was a law student, and they had four children. The man, who was completely unable to support his family, was desperate. His wife was trying to keep the family above water by traveling from town to town, teaching dressmaking, but they had given up on life, and no longer saw any reason to struggle further. They were planning to put an end to it all the next day by shooting themselves and their children.

We were able to take two of the children into our home, but this did not prevent catastrophe. Some months later, in another town, our worst fears were realized: we received a postcard notifying us that the man and the two children whom we had not taken in had been found dead, and that the woman was in critical condition, with a bullet wound in her head. Eberhard rushed for the next train and hurried to the house where the shooting had happened and from there to the hospital. It was a terrible situation. Eberhard was cross-examined by the court, which was naturally eager to establish who had committed the crime. This horrifying event shook us profoundly. We realized how little we were able to help others in desperate straits.

It was a very great joy to us that God gave us children. Emy-Margret was born on March 10, 1911, and Eberhard (we called him "Hardy") on August 18, 1912. To us, children were a wonderful confirmation of our marriage, and we received each one as a special gift.

In the spring of 1913, after Eberhard had held meetings in Halle, where we lived at the time, on the topic of following Christ, he was stricken with tuberculosis of the larynx and lungs. This threw all our plans into an upheaval. Eberhard's doctor advised a move into the mountain air, and we soon found the perfect refuge—a lodge high in the Alps of South Tirol. (Our second son, Heinrich, was born there two days before Christmas, 1913.)

Our move to the mountains was a step of daring: we had no regular income and no assurance of support. Our parents had hoped that Eberhard would stay at a sanatorium; they were willing to help us financially, and suggested that the rest of the family be divided up (they were worried the children might become infected). We, however, felt strongly that we should not be separated during a time like this, especially as the doctors had given us little hope for

Emmy with her first child, Emy-Margret, 1911.

Pichlerhof, the house in the Tirolean Alps where the Arnolds stayed from April 1913 to August 1914.

Eberhard's recovery. (He had seven infections in his lungs and had undergone two operations on his larynx).

As I had to look after a seriously ill husband and two (then three) young children, I asked my sister Else to come and live with us, which she did. From this time until her death in 1932, she was my right hand as well as Eberhard's secretary, and served us with loyalty and dedication.

Our time in the mountains gave us plenty of much-needed quiet contemplation and rest; indeed, our stay there was a gift of great importance for our future lives. As at other times of our life together, our reading and searching for deeper clarity and greater light became a source of strength. During this period, the first chapters of Eberhard's book *War: A Call to the Inner Land* were published in various magazines under the title "Greetings from the Mountains," as well as other articles. We also studied the early Anabaptist writings of Hans Denck, Balthasar Hubmaier, and others. This great movement – the most radical expression of the Reformation spirit – was centered in Switzerland and especially the Tirol, where Jakob Hutter, after whom the Hutterians were named, was born.

Thankfully the mountain retreat worked wonders, and gradually Eberhard recovered. In the majesty and grandeur of the Alps (and the jagged Dolomites, which faced our house) we rejoiced in the wonders of nature as never before: the rhythm of the seasons, the magnificent alpine flora, the rising of the sun from behind the peaks, and the red alpenglow of evening. For a long time after our return home, we continued to feel a deep longing for the closeness to nature that we had basked in during those eighteen months.

The time of quiet in our mountain retreat came to a sudden and abrupt end. During the night before August 2, 1914, the first day of German mobilization, we received a telegram summoning Eberhard to report immediately to his reserve unit. We had been aware that war was brewing, but when the news finally reached us, it came as a shock. Eberhard left for Halle the same day in an overflowing military train. From there he was immediately sent east in the direction of the front.

With war having been declared, mail now came to a complete standstill, and other avenues of communication were closed. We were without news from Eberhard. Since we had moved to the Tirol solely for Eberhard's sake, we—Else, Luise (a young German girl staying with us at the time), and I—considered taking the first possible train home.

Then on August 18 (Hardy's second birthday) news reached us that Italy had broken her alliance with Germany. Within hours we had packed the bare essentials and were on our way home. We managed to get on an overcrowded train leaving for Innsbruck the following day. Nobody could tell us how we would be able to travel on from there.

Normally the distance would have been covered in one night by express train, but the journey took us a full six days. We were traveling with three small children—Emy-Margret was three, Hardy just two, and Heinrich seven months. Thankfully our fellow travelers were friendly and helpful. When we finally reached my parents' home in Halle on the evening of August 24, we found out that Eberhard had been discharged from the army as physically unfit for active duty, and that he would be arriving that very day. What a homecoming it was, and what a reunion!

Everything was in the grip of war. Trainloads of wounded soldiers were already being transported from the battle lines, and cattle were being shipped to the front to feed the men. At home—in the railway stations and in the streets—people talked of nothing else. Great enthusiasm was evident everywhere. "Germany is surrounded by enemies from all sides. Let us fight! It is a just cause, and we will die for it and carry through to victory!"

Eberhard did not see things in such a rosy light. But when we looked around at the people who were so close to us, especially in Christian circles, we didn't know what to do. Husbands, brothers, and sons were at the front. What else could we do but go along with the general trend, supporting Germany and praying for victory? Hatred against the English was particularly strong, even among those who had experienced Christ. "We are German Christians, and God will give victory to our cause. God will punish England." This was the prevailing attitude, and it affected us too.

At this point we were living in a small rented house at Dölau on the outskirts of Halle. The house had a garden and bordered the Dölau heath, near a beautiful pine forest, which was good for Eberhard's health. It was a wonderful place for the children too, of course. Eberhard was continuing on his book *War: A Call to the Inner Land* (which eventually evolved into the book *Inner Land*).

Our friends in Halle who had been led to faith by Eberhard's witness were glad to have us back, especially as so many men had been called to the front. Already at this time we both had an uncanny feeling whenever we thought about the war. We began to ask ourselves, "How does all this fit in with the love of Jesus Christ? Where is the faith that was once so strong among our friends—the belief that the fellowship of faith, the alliance of all Christians, must stand high above all nationalism, above patriotic love for the fatherland? How can a Christian kill his brothers?"

When the Battle of the Marne was lost in 1915 and the tide began to turn against Germany, we grappled further with the question of what our duty was. Should Eberhard voluntarily enlist, or should he refuse?

With so many of their men at the front, the fellowship groups in Halle had been greatly weakened. In the more thoughtful quarters of the revival movement it was said that "we are all one in Christ," and that even in the present time Jesus was gathering his people out of all nations and races. We struggled to discern how this could fit with the attitude of most Christians toward war. Everyone was "Christian," yet the Germans were fighting the English, the French, and the Italians, and vice versa.

Gradually, and with much struggle, we came to feel that war could not be the will of God, and that the proclamation of the church as the mysterious Body of Christ (which we had heard so much about in those years) was being all but destroyed by it.

In the fall of 1915 we moved with our three children to Wilmersdorf, a suburb of Berlin. There, during the war, two more children were born to us: Hans-Hermann in December 1915, and Monika in February 1918. Like many wartime babies, both were physically weak.

In Berlin a new chapter of our life began. Eberhard worked with the Relief Committee for Prisoners of War in the literary department of the recently founded Furche Publishing House. The organization was headed by Georg Michaelis, Undersecretary of State and chairman of the German Student Christian Movement. As Eberhard had been both a member and director of the SCM in Halle, he was asked to be co-editor of its new monthly periodical, *Die Furche* (The Furrow).

The publishing house produced books, pamphlets, and art reproductions for prisoners of war and wounded soldiers in the military hospitals. These publications often had a German nationalistic slant; for instance, one was called *Der Heliand,* which loosely means, "the German Savior." This was done, of course, to foster morale among the combat troops and support the "just German cause." Everybody was expected to contribute his share toward victory; that was simply taken for granted.

Yet as time went on, more and more of the things put out by the Furche did not appeal to us, as we had the feeling they were a distortion of true Christian faith. There was a constant rush and pressure in the publishing house, and terrible tensions in the war work of the student movement. Eberhard continually pointed out that we had to find inner quiet—that we needed to concentrate on the inmost powers, especially amid the unrest of the times. But his advice was not appreciated. I can still remember Dr. Niedermeyer saying to him, "Dr. Arnold, there is no time for inwardness now. We are at war, *Herr Doktor,* at war!"

The fact that Germany was surrounded by enemies on all sides and had to fight them all simultaneously weighed heavily on us all, especially as it resulted in people feeling even more obligated to sacrifice themselves for the war effort. New German flags went up everywhere – in the streets, in public and private buildings – every time a new victory had been won against Russia, England, or Italy. On the other hand, the publicly displayed notices announcing the "heroic" deaths of soldiers and listing the wounded caused great shock and sorrow to many.

As the months went by, food became scarcer, until finally it was completely insufficient. Bread, sugar, fat, meat, and other food items could be bought only with ration cards, and the quantities became increasingly smaller. At one time the weekly rations per person were as follows: 4 lbs. bread; 4½ oz. sugar; less than ½ oz. butter, and a little more margarine. Only rutabagas (a variety of turnips) could be bought without ration cards. Ersatz coffee and many other things were made out of rutabagas.

Toward the end of the war many people were virtually starving. To make matters worse, there was tremendous inequality. Those who had money and connections were able to get hold of almost anything, while others went for days without food. In one apartment building, for instance, some had all they wanted, while others, like the caretaker and his wife, had nothing and had to send their children hungry to school. Yet all were expected to fight and give their lives for "the cause" on an equal basis.

Similar (if not worse) inequality existed at the front and behind the front lines, or so we heard. Officers lived in luxury while common soldiers had to survive with the bare minimum. There were also enormous contrasts between hospitals for ranking and non-ranking soldiers. Toward the end of the war, we began to hear slogans in the streets like, "Equal food and equal pay, and soon the war will fade away," or, "Wait until they come back home. Out there they learned how to steal." Looting, or "requisitioning," as it was called, was widespread. Naturally, none of this helped to raise the flagging spirit of patriotism.

During this time Eberhard paid frequent visits to army hospitals, where he had the freedom to come and go as a student counselor. He was often extremely depressed when he came home from such visits. He told us of the suffering, the anguish, the tormented consciences of many soldiers, and of various atrocities he had been told about.

Toward the end of the war, the questioning voice of our consciences became more audible and clear than ever. "How can it be possible for a Christian – indeed, for any human being – to take part in this mass murder?" "Is there no justice on this earth?" "What about the whole social order? How is it possible that all are fighting for the same goal, Germany's victory, and giving their lives for this while at the same time such blatant inequalities exist?"

When the hope for a victorious end to the war, which had upheld the people at least to some degree, was finally shattered, a great sadness – a hopelessness and despair – took hold of the masses. I can still see groups of people standing in front of the posters proclaiming the conditions of the armistice. They cried out: *"Wir sind kaputt!"* ("We are finished!") Even to the last minute it seemed many had cherished the vain hope that the war would somehow end in Germany's favor. The flags of victory, which had been kept flying right to the end, had strengthened this delusion. But now the truth was out. The Kaiser had abdicated and fled to Holland. Why didn't he stay with those who kept their soldier's vow to the bitter end, fighting and dying "for God, king, and fatherland"?

I will never forget the endless columns of soldiers that passed our house in those days – silent, bearded, and gray, their artillery pieces and field kitchens in tow. They were returning home defeated after four years at the front, and no one dared to say a word to them. Great sadness and mourning, disillusionment, emptiness, and fear were written on their faces.

The Wind Blows

Only a few days later, the streets of Berlin looked different again. It was November 9, 1918. Big trucks mounted with machine guns raced through the city, bedecked with the red banner of revolution. This flag was replacing the old black, white, and red one – the tricolor of the German Empire – on public buildings, outside private homes, and even on the Imperial Palace.

Gunfire could be heard everywhere. Columns of men still in military uniform marched boldly through the streets. Now all the pent-up suffering and hatred of the oppressed erupted. They had seen enough! There was sharp-shooting, brother against brother. Fighting took place throughout the city, and when we traveled by electric streetcar, we had to ride lying flat on the floor. Luckily the firing would cease twice a day, while the children were walking to and from school, picking their way through the streets on boards that had been laid across the trenches for them.

It is hard to describe the Revolution of 1918–1919. There had been plenty to indicate that unrest was brewing: people had been certain the war would be short, and that Germany would win it, and both hopes had proved to be utterly wrong. Then people had naïvely set their hopes on Wilson's Fourteen Points, only to have them dashed once they read the conditions of the armistice and saw what their leaders had agreed to.

At times we had the impression that Berlin had gone mad. In the center city we saw men with both legs and an arm gone, cranking hand organs with their one remaining limb. Everyone who passed by was drawn into a wild dance to their music. It was just crazy.

A few days later thousands gathered for the election of a new government in Berlin's biggest hall, the Zirkus Busch. Masses of people pushed their way inside, Eberhard and I among them. We

Folk dancing at the Tübingen conference, 1919. To Emmy's astonishment, Eberhard (second from L, with back to camera) returned home from this event in knee breeches and a loose tunic–the style of the youth movement.

were deeply shocked when someone from the crowd shouted, "Where was God in 1914? Were there any Christians at all then? The clergy are to blame, too; they even blessed the weapons!" A Chinese immigrant got up and shouted, "We converted to Christianity in our homeland, but what we have experienced here, what we have been taught–one nation fighting the next, men killing one another–has made us lose the faith your missionaries brought us. Christianity has become a mockery to the Hindus and Chinese!" Similar sentiments were expressed in other meetings as well.

When the actual election took place, nominees were suggested from all sides, from the Democrats to the Communists, who were represented by Karl Liebknecht and Rosa Luxemburg. (Both of them were brutally murdered later.) In the end Friedrich Ebert was elected president of Germany, but there was still no real political stability. For more than a year after the war the country went through one wave of violence and upheaval after another.

Something else happened in those days, something which had perhaps been evident even during the last period of the war. A great questioning began, mostly among those from the younger generation. Working class youth, artists, atheists, and Christians–all said,

"It cannot go on like this. What, after all, is the meaning of life?" This question came to us through our work at the Furche Publishing House and through the youth circles connected with it.

Naturally our searching soon brought us into contact with others, and we began to hold weekly open houses in our home to discuss the issues of the day. When the number of those attending grew to eighty, and then even one hundred, we began to hold meetings twice a week. Those who came included members from various branches of the youth movement, people from Christian circles, anarchists, atheists, Quakers, Baptists, artists, and representatives of the revival movement as well.

What did all these people have in common? Wasn't it just a great mixture, complete chaos? No. What brought us together was a single concern: "What shall we do? It can't go on like this any longer." There was no one who was able to give a clear-cut answer. So it happened that we came together in one common quest. People were expectant, open for any kind of direction or inspiration. Often we went on after midnight, until finally, after a prolonged struggle, a helpful insight drew us together and showed us the way forward.

Members of Sannerz with friends from "the Movement." In Eberhard's words (August 1918): "A new generation is arising to discover the highest and noblest calling of humanity, independent of all outside pressure and persisting in the face of everything base and hateful."

The writings of Tolstoy, Dostoyevsky, and Gustav Landauer spoke especially to our situation.

At that time the Furche brought out a book called *Die arme Schwester der Kaiserin* (The Poor Sister of the Empress). At one of our meetings Eberhard read a story, "Rachoff," from this book. In it a wealthy young Russian feels called by Christ to give his life in service to the poor. He leaves his parents' house, and on his wanderings comes face to face with the need and suffering of his people. Siding with the poor, he is marked by the State as a dangerous man and is cast into prison, where he suffers greatly himself.

Full of anticipation, we invited the author, Karl Josef Friedrich, to attend one of our open-house meetings and share his vision for a solution to the social problems we were struggling to confront. Perhaps he could advise us? When our guest arrived, however, he said only, "Yes, I wrote the book, and I was moved by that story, which is based on recorded facts. But I never said I would do the same thing myself." All who were present were greatly disappointed; they, like we, were looking for a way of action. There had been enough words, enough sermons, and books. What mattered now was deeds.

During the year following the armistice, a great number of conferences and retreats were organized across Germany, mostly by youth who were seeking a new direction for the future. Eberhard was invited to speak at many of them. One of the first was the Student Christian Movement conference on the Frauenberg near Marburg, which took place at Whitsun 1919. Here Eberhard addressed the gathering with his thoughts on the Sermon on the Mount. Reports of this conference, reviews of Eberhard's address, and testimonies of the effect his words had on listeners were published in several periodicals. In the magazine *Erfurter Führerblätter,* Erwin Wissman wrote:

> The focus of all that was said and thought was Jesus' Sermon on the Mount. Eberhard Arnold burned it into our hearts with a passionate spirituality, hammered it into our wills with prophetic power and the tremendous mobile force of his whole personality. This was the Sermon on the Mount in the full force of its impact, in its absolute and undiminished relevance, its unconditional absoluteness. Here there was no compromise. Whoever

wants to belong to this kingdom must give himself wholly and go through with it to the last! To be a Christian means to live the life of Christ. We are obligated by a burning challenge: the rousing summons to live, and the ominous warning, "He that takes the sword shall perish by the sword."

The discussions that followed were extremely lively, and from them a new stream of life, a vision of the future, came into our open-house meetings. Another conference was convened by the SCM in August 1919. The main topic of this one was "What is the attitude of a Christian to war and revolution? Can a Christian be a soldier?" Eberhard's answer was a clear "no." A report of this conference says:

> Eberhard Arnold recognizes the necessity of the new birth, and he says that this belongs to the [Christian] proclamation. Jesus recognized the authority of the state, but he spoke of the kingdom of God as something quite different: "The Christian must be a perpetual corrective of the state, a conscience of the state and its legislative task, a leaven, a foreign body in the sense of a higher value; but he cannot be a soldier, an executioner, or a police officer. It is our task to bear witness in word and deed and see to it that nothing in Jesus' words becomes confused. We must obey God rather than men! We must be a corrective element in this world!"

Eberhard's words struck the audience like lightning, and an animated argument ensued. It was more than an intellectual discussion; it was as if the very bottom had dropped out of things. Hermann Schafft contradicted Eberhard most vehemently. He as well as others represented that the State was "God's servant to punish evil and to foster good," as the apostle Paul expresses it. In a relative sense Eberhard agreed with this concept of the State; yet he urgently felt that the hour demanded more: it needed people who were willing to testify to Jesus' way of nonviolence.

After this there was another conference in Saarow, Brandenburg, where the same theme resulted in similar discussions and deliberations. Then on September 22–25, 1919, a meeting was held at Tambach in Thuringia. Here we experienced our first encounter with the Swiss Religious Socialists and met Karl Barth, who was one of the main speakers. The testimony of the Swiss, especially that of Karl

Barth, and his belief that "God is totally different from man" (i.e. man is insignificant) made a deep impression on the gathering.

I remember a small incident that occurred at the end of the conference. Otto Herpel, the chairman of the event and a member of our movement, had said something like, "Let us go home now and consider everything we have heard. We will meet again next year and see whether the God of old is still alive." At this the Swiss roared with laughter. How could we little human beings presume to discern such a thing? (Otto had actually meant to imply that God would surely be alive.) Offended, Otto left the meeting. After he was persuaded to come back, the Swiss publicly apologized for their outburst.

At Eberhard's places of work tensions were growing. At this time he was literary director of the Furche Publishing House, general secretary of the SCM, and an assistant with the German Student Service for Prisoners of War. In all three organizations, opinions were divided into two opposing camps. Everyone was aware of confusion among the youth, an effect of the turmoil and suffering of the war years. There were those who wanted to lead them back onto the beaten track of conventional church life and revivalist pietism. Others, Eberhard among them, believed that the young generation was looking on public events with an entirely different eye as a result of the war and the revolution. The young had learned a lesson from the blatant inequalities, the realities of military duty, and the whole war psychosis they had so painfully observed. They believed they must go an entirely different way, the way Jesus had spoken of – the way of the Sermon on the Mount.

The attitude of the latter group came to expression in several new publications of the Furche at that time, as well as in many of the manuscripts submitted to the publishing house, and this led to conflicts with those who wanted to stick with "old" ways and ideas. At about this time we became acquainted with the people of *Der Christliche Demokrat* (The Christian Democrat), a journal we later took over under the name *Das neue Werk* (The New Work). We quickly grew close to these friends who were seeking new paths and, like us, were willing to travel them. All were determined: the old and the rotten could not be part of a new life!

Meanwhile the struggling and searching continued in our open house meetings. The Sermon on the Mount was both our direction and our goal, but there were other voices that made themselves heard too. Some said, "It is impossible to live up to that today! There will always be rich and poor. You can't eliminate competition. Everyone has to do the best he can with what he has. Otherwise people would soon take advantage of each other's generosity." Yet we could hardly ignore the contrast between this attitude and Jesus' words: "If someone wants to take your jacket, give him your coat as well. Live like the lilies in the fields and the birds in the air. Have no enemies. Love your enemies. Do good to them!" And so we continued to struggle. People asked us, "But what would you do if somebody carried off your furniture?" or, "What if somebody were to rape or kill your own wife in front of you? How could you love such a person?"

Our circle continued to grow. As a result of the various conferences, members of both the youth movement and the workers' movement came to us. For these young men and women, the longing of the Free German Youth as expressed at the Hohe Meissner Conference of 1913 was still alive, and it urged them to action: "We want to be free to build up and determine our own lives in a truthful and genuine way." The workers' movement was fighting for freedom, equality, and brotherhood: "We know no differences. We know no enemies. All disparity is caused by the upper classes; the lower classes must no longer be forced to follow their example!"

Through reading the Sermon on the Mount, we grew more concerned with finding a practical way to express our inward longings. But what should the new life be like? Many suggestions were made. It became more and more unbearable for us to continue in the old middle-class way of life. We discussed a number of possibilities: folk schools, cooperatives, and land settlements of various kinds. Eberhard and I had the idea of buying a gypsy trailer, or even several, and traveling from village to village, from town to town this way, with our family and anyone who wanted to join us. We would make music, speak to people and try to encourage them, and teach our children as we went along. We would travel without a destination, staying in a particular place only as long as our help was needed and accepted by the war widows, the children, the sick, and the poor, whose homes we would help to rebuild. Many people were attracted to this vision.

A short time later, in the same open-house meetings, we read from the Book of Acts, chapters 2 and 4, about Pentecost.

Now the multitude of those who believed were of one heart and soul, and no one said that any of the things he possessed were his own, but they held everything in common. There was not a needy person among them, for as many as were possessors of lands or houses sold them, and brought the proceeds of what was sold... Distribution was made to each as had need. (Acts 4:32–35)

Here, we felt, was an answer to our seeking and questioning: community of faith, community of love, community of goods – all born from the energy of that first love. Perhaps we would be an itinerant community, in trailers or on foot, or maybe we ought to build up a settlement. Whatever form it took, we now knew we had to be messengers of a church aflame with love.

We are like fires through the darkness burning
And though we may burn for a single night,
Yet joy upon joy in wealth o'erflowing
And light to the land our fire has brought.

Soon we began to look for actual possibilities. Working-class friends favored a settlement in the country, which would give people like themselves a chance to visit us there, away from the industrial towns. We ourselves were contemplating a house in the city, in collaboration with the fellowship we had helped to create in Halle in 1907. This group envisioned a large settlement house or hall; and they were ready to put one at our disposal, right in the city's worst slum.

Eberhard did a lot of traveling as he looked for a suitable place. Then a letter from Georg Flemmig, a teacher from Schlüchtern, suggested possibilities in that region. His letter came as a call to us, a challenge to live in the manner of the early church. Flemmig told us that groups who lived in the same spirit of expectation were to be found in every part of the country; that the movement was not confined to our own circle. So Eberhard traveled to Schlüchtern to get acquainted with the group gathered there.

Near Schlüchtern Eberhard found several possibilities for a new community, for instance, the Ronneburg, an old castle ruin near Gelnhausen. Friedrich Wilhelm Cordes, a well-to-do man from Hamburg and a good friend of ours, sobered Eberhard's enthusiasm for this project considerably when he said, "How will you find someone who knows how to go about rebuilding such a place?" Yet Eberhard remained attracted to the castle because of its "spiritual" history. Here, at the time of Count Zinzendorf in the eighteenth century, a group of people had lived in community of faith and goods, and Zinzendorf, who was exiled from his native Saxony on account of his faith, had himself participated. The Ronneburg plan was soon given up, but we were to visit the castle often in the future.

Two more conferences took place during this period before the beginning of our own community. First, we had sent invitations to a number of interested friends to meet with us on the Inselsberg in the Thuringian Forest. These people shared our concern to create a new way of life, and with them we climbed the mountain with our rucksacks, guitars, and violins, making music and singing together.

On the way we stopped for an informal gathering. It was good to talk things over out in nature, in the beautiful springtime weather. Between meetings we sang old and new folk songs: "O lovely, flowering Maytime," "Winter is past," and many others. We often sang one about the blue flower – youth's symbol of beauty, truth, purity, and longing:

> And deep in the wood there is blooming
> A flower of heavenly blue;
> And just to win this flower
> We'll travel the wide world through.
> The trees are a-rustle, the stream murmurs low,
> And he who the blue flower seeking would go
> Must be a wanderer too!

Everyone sensed that hidden in nature lay a mystery: God. Most had not experienced God or had lost sight of him – if not through disillusionment with the established churches, then through the terrible experiences of war. Out in nature, however, we felt something of a true quest for the unknown God and a sense of great reverence for him when we gathered and sang together.

A quiet song, a peaceful song,
A song so tender and fine,
Like a cloudlet that over the blue sky sails,
Like a cotton grass blown in the wind.

Behind all this stood a Creator whose name we hardly dared pronounce, it had been so misused and distorted.

In the course of these conferences we not only experienced nature and the mystery hidden behind it. We also worked hard and searched eagerly for concrete alternatives to the old life we had rejected. Separate groups were formed to tackle specific tasks, exploring ways and means to start a country or folk school, to create a social work center, and so forth. One group considered the founding of a settlement on the land, and many participated in this. They emphasized a return to agriculture as the healthiest basis for such a venture.

Eberhard had already explored the idea of settlements for himself, and summarized them in an article entitled, "The Fellowship of Families and Settlement Life." He spoke of five distinct areas in which youth could band together to build up something new: farming and gardening, education and schooling, publishing and outreach, housing (in the form of a children's home) for war orphans, and arts and crafts work. Many responded to his vision, but most saw its realization as something for the distant future.

At the end of the Inselsberg conference, Marie Buchhold, who had helped start a women's community near Darmstadt, stood up and said, "There have been enough words. Let us see some action now!" With this we parted from one another, firmly resolved to go into action. We descended the mountain with the joyful song:

When we're striding side by side
And the songs of old are singing,
Echoes from the woods are ringing,
Every heart in joy's believing
With us goes a new time.

Another important conference took place in Schlüchtern in the late spring of 1920, at Whitsun. In conjunction with others, we had invited dozens of interested youth from various groups to join us. We left Berlin at five o'clock in the morning on a *Bummelzug* (slow train) – the kind that stops at every station – and traveled fourth class, because it was the cheapest. We were due to arrive in Schlüchtern at eight in the evening. With us in the train were members of the Free German Youth, the young men in shorts and loose tunics, and the young women in simple, bright-colored dresses. Many had violins, flutes, or guitars, and we sang one song after another. Our other traveling companions sat along the walls of the compartment, but we stood in the middle and sang, for there were not enough seats to go around.

When we arrived at our destination, we climbed to the top of a hill and lit our Whitsun fire. As the blaze threw its light over the fields below, we thought of how it symbolized the burning up of the old and the coming of something new. We thought, too, of the flame of which Jesus had spoken, "I came to cast fire upon the earth;

At a Whitsun conference in May 1920 near Schlüchtern, northeast of Frankfurt, Eberhard Arnold (one of the organizers) spoke on "the mystery of the early church." One month later the Arnolds left Berlin and began to practice community of goods.

and would that it were already kindled!" It was as if he himself were speaking to us.

Later we sat under the lofty beech trees and listened as different people spoke, and participated in the ensuing discussions. Afterward, our heads buzzing with all the ideas, we danced together – folk dances that expressed our feeling of community – and sang folk songs, and songs of love and nature. Our dances were a truly religious experience, as Eberhard wrote in one of his poems:

> Spirit-gripped, / Move as one.
> Circle round, / Center-bound!

Between meetings we cooked our meals on open fires in the beech wood. Everyone unpacked what provisions he had in his rucksack, and all shared the simple food. Sometimes we gathered in little groups around the cooking pots; at other times we sat on the ground in a large circle, the girls with garlands of wildflowers in their hair, the boys in their shorts and tunics. Outward formality and social conventions had been cast off. A spirit of joy and comradeship was alive among us.

What filled us most throughout those Whitsun days was the desire to carry something new into the world, to blaze a trail for the kingdom of God, to proclaim the message of peace and love. The example of St. Francis of Assisi, with his love for people and animals, meant a great deal to us.

One morning the English Quaker John Stephens suggested that we have a silent meeting – "You Germans still talk far too much." He began by explaining the true significance of such a meeting, and suggested that we should sit together in silence for perhaps half an hour or so, in order to listen to the Spirit. Seconds after he had ended an elderly professor from Frankfurt rose to his feet and made quite a long speech, whereupon John stood up and said simply, "Hush." The professor reacted touchily, and we all burst out laughing!

The topics we discussed were of great importance to everyone. Above all we were concerned with the movement of the Spirit of Pentecost two thousand years ago and its consequences ever since. We talked about the "new life," and about *eros* and *agape* – human love and divine love. We all felt something was breaking in upon us.

One day we hiked to a "life-reform" settlement called the Haberts-hof in nearby Elm, to see what the "new life" might look like. This communal settlement was begun by Max and Maria Zink, a couple from southern Germany, a year before our own new beginning got under way. We city dwellers were deeply impressed by the simple life of these people up there on a hillside—and by their complete lack of pretension, which showed itself in their adoption of a plain peasant-style garb. Eberhard and I began to feel that perhaps our own future community should take a similar outward form.

While sitting together in the evenings, we often sang Matthias Claudius's song, "The moon has gently risen." We never ended without singing the *Schlüchterner Lied ("Kein Schöner Land"),* which speaks of gathering in the beauty of the countryside. On one occasion about a year later, after we had stood in a circle and sung this song to close a meeting, someone spontaneously added a new verse:

> You brothers know what makes us one;
> For us shines bright another Sun.
> For him we're living, t'ward him we're striving,
> The church at one.

It was at the end of that Whitsun conference of 1920 that Eberhard and I and some others walked to the nearby village of Sannerz, to look at a house we had been told about. The building, a large brick one, was standing empty. It belonged to a certain Konrad Paul, who had built it with money he had made in America. It took us about two hours to reach Sannerz, as we chose a route over the hills and also rested on the way. Our first stop was in the little village inn, where we were well received and given a good meal. Afterwards we went across the road to have a look at the villa, as it was known—a building that was to become significant for us and for many other people in the future.

Herr Paul was friendly and accommodating. The house seemed suitable for our purpose, with its fifteen rooms, a kitchen, and a number of attic rooms that could be remodeled as dwellings. There were cattle sheds, pigsties, and poultry houses, a sizable orchard, and even some fields suitable for farming. On the whole, the place struck us as a little too middle-class, at least compared with the Habertshof, which seemed much more appropriate for the simple life we had in mind. Yet at that time there were not too many choices. In a Germany too poor to be able to import produce, farmers were seldom willing to part with their land, and this was a rare find.

We returned to Berlin with the question of purchasing the property unresolved, but began to pack anyway. We had no place to go, yet we were certain we could no longer stay in Berlin, and we felt that if we acted in simple faith and trust, we would be guided clearly.

Beginning at Sannerz

Our relationship with the Furche Publishing House was becoming increasingly difficult. Articles and manuscripts that we and our friends found challenging and suitable for publication were not appreciated (and even turned down) by people in influential positions, and the resulting tensions frustrated us at a time when we felt the need around us and the Spirit calling us to action. Just at this juncture, friends at Schlüchtern asked Eberhard if he would be willing to take charge of a new publishing house they were planning to start, the *Neuwerk Verlag.*

No, there was no financial basis of any kind, either for starting this proposed business venture or for buying the villa at Sannerz and realizing our dream of a community house. But that made no difference. We decided it was time to turn our backs on the past and start afresh in full trust. Well-meaning friends shook their heads. What an act of rash irresponsibility for a father of five little children to go into the unknown just like that! Frau Michaelis, the wife of the former Chancellor of the Reich, visited me and offered to help the children and me should my husband really take this "unusual" step. After talking with me, she reported to a mutual friend: "*She* is even more fanatical than *he* is! There is nothing we can do."

Our departure from Berlin on June 21, 1920 came about very suddenly. Monika, our youngest, then two years old, was sickly because of wartime malnourishment during her infancy. The same was true of our youngest son, Hans-Hermann, then four years old, but (like Monika) too weak to walk. When, in addition to this, Monika became ill with a gastric infection, our pediatrician advised us to move immediately to the country with her, so that she could have fresh milk, eggs, honey, and good bread. We sent a telegram to the owner of the village inn in Sannerz, and announced our arrival for the next day.

Thus Eberhard and I left for Sannerz with our little Monika early that Sunday morning, the day of the summer solstice. Our four other children followed a few days later, accompanied by our helper Suse Hungar, a woman from the Salvation Army, and another woman, Luise Voigt. Both had volunteered to come with us, at least for a while. My sister Else stayed behind to wind up our affairs with the publishing house. Friendly Mr. Lotzenius, the innkeeper, had three little rooms ready for us to use during the summer, which he had been using for harness making in summer and apple storage in winter.

Earlier, of course, we had set our hopes on Konrad Paul's house on the other side of the road. Now, however, the owner hesitated, saying he was not sure whether he wanted to sell or lease the place after all. More probably he was hopeful that if he left us in a state of suspense, he could command a better price.

Some money had been offered to us—30,000 marks (which still had some value in those days) for the purpose of founding a "community modeled after the early church." The donor was our

The barn in Sannerz where the Arnolds rented three small rooms in the summer of 1920, after leaving their home in exclusive Berlin-Steglitz.

friend Kurt Woermann of the Hamburg-Africa Line. There was also our life insurance policy which we planned to sell, though this would not bring us much cash. Yet we were determined to burn all our bridges and put our trust entirely in God, like the birds of the air and the flowers in the field. This trust was to be our foundation – the surest foundation, we felt, on which to build.

After several weeks we finally reached an agreement with Herr Paul. We were to sign a rental agreement for ten years, and buy all the farm equipment and furniture on the place as well as all the livestock, consisting of four cows, several goats, pigs, and chickens. We had to make a down payment of 30,000 marks, including the rent for a year in advance.

Right from the start the house was flooded with a constant stream of guests, most of them from the youth movement and its branches. For accommodations, we sent them to find sleeping quarters in the haylofts of neighboring farms. What was more difficult was finding work for everyone: the only real job on hand was gathering and chopping firewood from the forest behind the house for use in the kitchen and laundry.

Little by little we were able to take possession of the "Neuwerk House," as we named it. Three front rooms on the ground floor were available right away, and we used them for offices and for our

Eberhard and Emmy nicknamed Konrad Paul's villa "Sonnherz" (sunheart). The nerve center of the Neuwerk branch of the youth movement, it housed the Arnolds and their growing community from 1920 to 1927.

publishing work. By December we had the use of the whole house, as we had finally been able to get all the money together. We celebrated with great enthusiasm, singing one Advent song after another, and even writing a new song—"In holy waiting we're at home"—as an expression of our joy. We sang it for the first time under Else's window on her birthday, December 13.

At six o'clock every morning we gathered around the kitchen fire, where the oatmeal was cooking. We sat in silence, listening—all seven of us who had remained together to go this new way, after the crowds of summer guests had left us. A powerful spirit of expectation was living in us; it seemed to us as if the kingdom would break in any day! We who were living in community, together with those who came to stay with us, all shared this outlook. Who knew what the next day might bring? After this we went to work—in the office, in the garden, in the children's room (we were teaching them at home) and elsewhere around the house.

Simplicity—poverty for the sake of Christ—was like an article of faith with us. How could we, who wanted to share the suffering of the masses in those post-war years, keep anything for ourselves? That is why we shared everything in common, giving away all we had to those who wanted to serve the same spirit of love with us.

Another matter of great importance to us was chastity—the purity of each individual—and marriage as a symbol of the unity of God with the church. As weak human beings, we were conscious that a disciplined life would be possible only through faith in Christ and through giving ourselves completely to him, but we counted it a joy to strive for this.

During the winter months we did not have as many visitors, which made it possible to cement the bonds within our little group more deeply. But as soon as spring returned, guests began to pour through the house once more. Young people who were hiking in the countryside to enjoy nature dropped in on us by the hundreds. During that year some two thousand came, staying with us at least one night. Among them were students, members of Christian groups, *Wandervögel* (an informal movement of wandering youth known as "birds of passage"), anarchists, atheists, and others who had turned their backs on the existing social order.

Most of our guests came on foot. Who had money for train travel in those days anyway? Nobody wanted it either. Some who came did not want to use coal or tools, since these were produced at the expense of miners and factory workers and filled the coffers of people who had never done honest work themselves.

Nearly all of them felt community was "the" solution: the community of the people, the fellowship of nations, harmony with nature and peace with humanity as a whole–finally, union with God and with the Body of Christ. We used to talk together until the early hours of the morning. Many times our discussions became quite heated, but we were usually able to end on a harmonious note. Often we would end with a quiet dance, moving in a circle as we sang.

There were moments in these gatherings when something came to us which was not from ourselves, nor from those who were visiting us. This was especially true in encounters with people who were burdened or tormented by demonic powers. As Eberhard described it years later:

> Among us–those who were living together and those who came to share the experience–the Holy Spirit brought us face to face with the presence of God in our gatherings and meetings. The rooms in Sannerz were filled with a power in those early days, a power that did not originate from us who were living there, nor from those who were our guests. It was a power from God that visited us, an invisible power that surrounded us. In this way we were able to understand Pentecost as the rushing wind of the spirit visiting the expectant church with the Holy Spirit. This wonderful mystery brought the church into being. Here no one's own will or word could be spoken or added, not even the word of a so-called leader or of a so-called opposition. The voice comes from the cloud, and man is silent. However, this does not mean that only those who confess Christ, who confess that they are converted or reborn Christians, are touched by the cloud. The very opposite is the case. We experienced many times that the hidden Christ is revealed through people who insist that they have no faith. Christ visits all people, long before they have found unity with him. We believe that the light of Christ illuminates every person who comes into this world.

For those of us who experienced this beginning, the "first love" remains unforgettable. Even recently I have met people who were present in those formative days; they have told me it had an impact on their whole future. It is quite clear, of course, that nobody can live off memories from the past. Today, too, the spirit lives, calling people as in the time of John the Baptist: "Repent, for the kingdom of heaven is at hand!" Jesus calls men and women to follow him, to leave everything in search of the one precious pearl. Here and there this is happening now. Yet for every person, the time of his first zeal and love will always be significant, and in times of weakness he will be able to turn back to it, as to a reservoir of strength.

From the beginning we did not want to be the founders of a work of our own. Community can never be founded; it can only be given as a gift of the Spirit. We simply wanted to live as brothers and sisters, and take into our midst anyone else who wanted the same. It became obvious many times, however, that people who wanted to follow their own ideas were not ready to go this way. There were clashes in the daily life, and in our discussions; now and then a guest would even disturb our inner meetings, in which case we might have to ask him to leave. In fact, it rarely happened that a person had to

Like this mealtime on the front porch, every gathering at Sannerz was signifi-cant–not only for members, but for the thousands of guests who were drawn to the new spirit there.

be *sent* away; opposing spirits generally seemed to sift and separate themselves, even if it did not always happen quickly.

Though daylight hours were dedicated to the work, evenings belonged to guests, and to talks with them. As I mentioned earlier, our encounters could be quite heated. It was not unusual, on the other hand, for an argument to bring everyone to silence. Then something new and unexplainable, something that united us all, broke in.

Our guests were always a diverse lot, but there were some who were downright peculiar. One who impressed us most was a certain Hans Fiehler, who called himself "Hans-in-Luck." Wearing a red woolen cap, shorts, and a red waistcoat with "Hans-in-Luck" in bold letters across the back, he hiked through the countryside with two violins. One was a good Italian instrument that he had bought in Italy; the other a tin one he had obtained from the gypsies. Hans-in-Luck had four ocarinas (pottery whistles shaped like a bird): the "great-grandmother," "grandmother," "mother," and "child."

When he entered a village or town playing his ocarinas, Hans-in-Luck was soon followed by a large crowd of children, whom he gathered in the square. He always had something to tell them, a message to proclaim. Usually he would tell them stories about heaven and earth, about mankind's future and the future of creation – that in a time to come, the whole earth would be like heaven! Nearly all of these children had experienced terrible things in the war; they knew hunger and want, and many had lost father or mother or both. But when Hans formed a circle with them, and they sang and danced, their joy knew no bounds.

Hans-in-Luck regarded Sannerz as a home and made lengthy stays with us, and his outlook affected all of us. "Why," he would ask, "do we always speak of the good old times? Why do we say, 'Once upon a time there was…', instead of 'One day it will come about, that…'? Why do we say 1920 and so on? Why not 80 before 2000?" We took this expectant attitude toward the future, and his eagerness for the coming of God's reign on earth, with all earnestness, and it stirred us deeply.

Once he had the children help him plant a "tree of the year 2000"–a little plum – on the lawn in front of the house; afterwards we all danced around it, singing one of his spontaneous child-like compositions. On another occasion he got us to march through the village with him, carrying paper lanterns, and singing together to the accompaniment of his instruments: "Through the gates of the new age, on we march with singing!"

Several times Hans-in-Luck came into conflict with the authorities. During one summer he had rented an observation tower in the Harz Mountains, where he worked as a guide and sold souvenirs. One time he left the tower for lunch and fixed a verse on the door: "Hans-in-Luck his stomach fills. Do the same—beyond the hills." When he returned to find a crowd of people smoking and drinking, he lost his temper and set fire to the building. Jailed for several days on account of this incident, he wrote to us from his cell, "From the little attic room of a *Wandervogel*…I send you my heartfelt greetings."

Hans-in-Luck with a friend in 1925–or as he would say, "75 before 2000."

In 1924, at a time when inflation was at its peak and many people were starving, Hans-in-Luck approached an army general in one of the large cities (I forget which one) and made the following proposal: If you want to restore your good standing with the populace, take your field kitchens into the city and feed the poor. I'll stand by and make a film of it all. Amazingly, the plan really came off! Hans-in-Luck stood there with his camera, commanding the general, "Stand up smartly!" "Dish it up yourself!" and so on. Only after everything had been served was it "discovered" that there was no film in the camera. Fortunately for Hans-in-Luck, the crowd was on his side, and he got away with the prank.

With so many hundreds of people coming in and out of it, our house at Sannerz began to look rather shabby. One day the landlord came and demanded that we repaint it. Naturally we had no money for such a project, though Hans-in-Luck and another guest said they would do the work if we would buy the paint. And do the work they did, though not quite as we might have imagined it. Downstairs in the front hall they painted a huge picture of a rising sun, and of someone ringing a bell: "Bim, bam, bom; Spring of the nations, come!" On the staircase wall a mural emerged: the whole household dancing and skipping after Eberhard, who led them gaily onward and upward. Everyone found a caricature of himself—even the geese had not been forgotten! On another wall was painted the melody of the song: "Let our hearts be always happy," and around the notes were children dancing. Hans-in-Luck was still adding the finishing touches as some well-to-do visitors arrived, looked at his painting, and asked him in astonishment, "Where are you from?" "From a lunatic asylum," came the cheerful reply.

Many years later, in a book about resistance to the Third Reich, we read that Hans-in-Luck had been imprisoned by his brother, then Mayor of Munich, and tortured for his beliefs in future world peace. After the war I wrote to acquaintances in Munich in an effort to trace him, but I was not able to learn anything. It seems our dear friend had disappeared, having suffered the same fate as so many others who raised their voices in protest during that dark time.

Something that always struck me about the first years at Sannerz was the way men and women who had lost all faith as a result of war and revolution were able to experience the Creator through their contact with nature. Outdoors, in the blowing of the wind, in the beautiful countryside, and in the simple life of shared work and leisure, they experienced the reality of the Spirit, which brings God close to us. For many this led to a newfound faith in Christ, though there were just as many of our guests who refused to have anything to do with religion.

All sorts of unusual people came to visit us: there was the opera singer who sang to us for a whole evening, and the family who turned up, each dressed like a different wildflower. All they would say was, "We come from the woods; we live in the woods; we return to the woods." Some of our vegetarian visitors were so fanatic that they would eat nothing but raw vegetables or fully ripened fruit. One certain young man decided he could not, in good conscience, eat anything at all, and ended up dying of starvation.

Sometimes tramps visited us, tipsy, but attracted by the communal music-making and singing. Everyone was welcome, and we tried to concern ourselves with each who came. This was how Karl Gail landed up with us one day—drunk, but very much taken with what he saw and experienced. "I cannot stay with you," he said; "I am a wicked man..." In the days that followed Karl told us the whole sad story of his life as an alcoholic, and the roots of his great need. Luckily we were able to encourage him to stay on at Sannerz, which he did, though every few months he would lapse into his old ways and leave. When he came home, completely drunk and lamenting that he was not worthy of us, he would ask our forgiveness and promise, once again, to mend his ways. This went on for years, until Hitler came to power, after which Karl left for good. Sadly we never heard from him again.

All in all, our life in community was a joyful one, driven by our expectation of a new future. This was especially so during the first two years. Each day together was an occasion for festivities, and we never missed a chance to celebrate. When we bought a cow or a goat, for instance, we decorated it with wreaths of wildflowers and led it through the village, singing together. It was the same with our work: Whether we had finally picked all the rocks from a newly-rented field, or finished hoeing the beans, peas, and potatoes; whether we had preserved the last of the autumn fruit or brought in an especially good harvest of vegetables—each completed task was an opportunity for fun and fellowship. Everybody joined in, even those who were overburdened with work in the office because of the many books we brought out in those first years. Often people from the village were invited too.

Among the books we prepared for publication during this time were a collection of Tolstoy's letters; Joan Mary Fry's *Sacrament of Life* in German translation; Goldschmidt's *Die Rassenfrage* (a book on racism); Zinzendorf's *Vom Glauben und Leben* (On Faith and Life); Blumhardt's *Vom Reich Gottes* (The Kingdom of God); and

Die Nachfolge Christi (Discipleship of Christ). There was also *Junge Saat: Lebensbuch einer Jugendbewegung* (Young Seed: Life-Book of a Youth Movement), an anthology edited by Eberhard Arnold and Normann Körber; Georg Flemmig's *Dorfgedanken* (Village Musings) and *Hausbacken Brot* (Homemade Bread); and *Legenden,* a little book of legends. In addition, we put out the journal *Das neue Werk* every month.

When I think back to those days, I feel it was a foretaste of what we can expect in a much greater and more perfect measure in the future. The thought makes me shiver, but I feel a deep joy and thankfulness for it too. Something of eternity was living among us; something that made us forget the limits of time and space.

Now and again miracles, as one might call them, occurred. It is difficult to speak about these events, for they came about quite simply and unobtrusively. Demonic powers retreated right in our meetings; sick people became well again, almost unnoticed; other things happened that cannot be humanly explained. We did not regard such occurrences as being unusual, however – they seemed a natural part of God's working among us. A short time before he died, Eberhard said to me, "God gave us much, but he would have given much more if we had had more strength." Yes, it all happened in spite of us – in spite of our insufficiencies and incapabilities.

All of our special holidays – Advent, Christmas, Easter, and Whitsun – were celebrated communally, and their meaning stayed with us throughout the year, not only on specific dates. During Advent each year we rehearsed a Christmas play together, and then took it from village to village. Conditions were primitive. Dressing rooms were unheated even though it was winter; and the halls we used (which we decorated with fragrant spruce branches) were rarely heated beforehand, if at all. If there was a stove, we had to fetch the firewood from the forest ourselves. We never charged for admission. We remembered Jesus' words, "Freely you have received, freely give." All the same, we placed an empty sack at the door, and into this our audience – almost all poor peasants – put anything they could afford to give: eggs, a cut of ham, sausage, or a loaf of bread. After walking home through the deep snow, we prepared a meal from these gifts—a rare feast indeed.

One beautiful Christmas Eve tradition was our walk into the forest on Albing Mountain. There, in a sheltered spot, we stood in a circle around a small, candle-lit spruce and sang one carol after another. After the Christmas story was read, each of us took a candle from the tree and made a procession down the slope, protecting our candles from the wind as we walked. If someone's flame died, it was rekindled by another's—a symbol of the mutual love and help we strove for in our daily life.

Each year old songs were rediscovered and added to our repertoire; I particularly loved Martin Luther's chorale, "Now be Thou praised, O Christ Jesu" with the verse:

Eternal light doth now appear
To the world both far and near;
At darkest midnight it shines bright,
And makes us children of His light.

When sung in Bach's arrangement, it sounded to me like the music of the spheres. There was also the old hymn, "Come, give now to Christ all honor." When Eberhard suggested that one at the end of a meeting, he would take my arm and lead us singing through the house. Otto Salomon's "Lo, a light is in the East" and Eberhard's "Christmas night, O night of nights" were written in those days. The latter expressed the essence of our longing: "Make us poor, just as thou wert, Jesus; poor through thy great love!"

It was in one of those first years that we held our first silent nativity scene. Eberhard was Joseph; I represented Mary and held a bundle with a bright light inside. Children dressed as angels stood around us, each with a candle; then came shepherds, kings, and a throng of onlookers bowing in homage.

In later years, our silent crib scene became a central part of our celebration, taking place in a cattle stall or other simple shed, and often being the only gathering we had on Christmas Eve. The sharing of presents with its accompanying merriment and childlike joy was saved for Christmas Day itself.

One December we learned a simple drama based on the parable of the ten virgins, and played it in several of the surrounding villages. At each performance the audience was gripped by its serious message—and we were too. Rehearsals were like worship meetings. Though normally we avoided religious language and pious talk, we could not do so now; nor did we want to, for the lines in this play were expressions of genuine reverence. Not only the adults but also our children were sensitive during our practices. As we realized in later years, they took in the significance of much that went on, even though they may not have understood it.

Naturally the children (including those underprivileged ones we had taken into our house) also produced their own little plays, and did so wholeheartedly. In the same way they were very fond of their own favorite childlike Christmas songs.

Holy Week was another special time for us, as we gathered inwardly to consider the events of two thousand years ago. On Holy Thursday we usually prepared a kid (we could not afford lamb) for our evening meal; then we sang many songs about Jesus' last hours on this earth. Good Friday was generally observed in silence—it was a day for each individual to think on the meaning of Christ's death— though we did read the story of the crucifixion aloud at a meeting in the morning. On Saturday we assembled in silence to remember Jesus' burial. Often we sang only one song:

> Oh sadness, oh suffering of heart,
> Shall we not lament?
> God the Father's only child
> Is carried to the grave.

> Oh greatest need,
> God himself is dead.
> On the cross he died,
> Thus gaining for us
> The kingdom of heaven
> By his love.

Easter Sunday was a day of joyful celebration: evil, sin, separation, and death had been overcome through the resurrection of Christ! Often we climbed up to the Weiperz Cross before daybreak, at three o'clock in the morning. Here a fire had been prepared the day before. After it was lit, we walked around it, slowly and silently. Sometimes this or that one might briefly express what was on his heart. At the rising of the sun we sang many beautiful songs, and then the Easter story was read aloud from the one of the Gospels.

Our Easter meetings were very deep meetings. Our youngest children were often present, but they were hardly ever a disturbance – they were so absorbed in the experience. Guests were also with us, especially young men and women from the youth movement. Because of their reverence for "that which lies behind it," as they themselves put it, they rarely disturbed our meetings in any way. Yes, often they jumped through the fire with us, singly or in pairs, after the flames had died down. This rediscovered tradition was a language not of words, but of action, and it came out of an inner experience. There had been too many spoken words in times past!

Whitsuntide was "our" feast more than any other: after all, it was the spirit of Pentecost and the first church in Jerusalem that had inspired us to go this way of life. Not that we wanted to imitate anything. This cannot be done in any case, for what is of the Spirit should never be copied. Yet it is as impossible to found a church by oneself – without the Spirit, that is – as to marry without a partner.

Enthusiastic folk dancing at Sannerz gave expression to the joy of the new life, free from the social conventions of the bourgeoisie.

And hadn't it been at the unforgettable Whitsun conference of 1920 in Schlüchtern that we had experienced such an outpouring of new energy and love?

At Whitsun 1921 we held a conference in Sannerz; our theme was the way of love and its freedom. During these days we were led together especially deeply by reading the First Letter of John. Early in the morning, before breakfast, we climbed the Albing Mountain with our musical instruments. We wanted to be led and strengthened for the day ahead by the words of the apostle of love!

There was, of course, the usual mix of elements. One morning during the conference, Max Schulze-Sölde, a guest, stepped into our meeting and implored the spirit to fall down upon us from the beech leaves above. "What are you saying?" someone cried out. "Is that the spirit we want to come over us?" There was considerable unrest among all those present, and Eberhard, who was not the main speaker, quietly led Max away. Soon, however, we were able to continue our common seeking undisturbed.

Early morning meetings at Sannerz had a deep meaning for us, and not just at conferences. Anyone who was at peace with God and his brothers and sisters could take part; those who were not stayed away. At that time we wore rings: women and girls a silver headband and the men an open ring on their finger. Both symbolized our belonging to an open circle. The idea had come from Georg Flemmig's "early church" movement in nearby Schlüchtern, a group we felt very close to in those days. As with our meetings, anyone who felt disunited from the rest of our circle did not wear the ring or band.

The genuineness of the form, as it comes into being through unity, through the feeling of being one, was very important for our communal life, whether it concerned our meetings and meals, our products (i.e. books, crafts, and furniture), or our clothes. We always preferred the simplest and plainest. Our goal was not dullness, though – far from it. Whenever possible, we used the bold colors of the rainbow which, when blended, create the white color of light. Everything had its inner significance.

During the summer of 1921 we had dozens of guests from the working class. Many of them challenged us to live even more simply – to give up everything that was not absolutely necessary – for the sake of love for the poor. Eberhard and I had known of the Swiss religious socialist Hermann Kutter since 1912, when we had read his books, and we had tried to live more simply since then. But we did not realize how "bourgeois" we still appeared to the poorest of the poor, and we were grateful for their efforts to help us continue on the way we had chosen.

Among those who visited us that summer were Theo Spira, a writer influenced by early Quakerism, and Martin Buber, the well-known Jewish philosopher. Martin Buber happened to come just on the day that Suse Hungar was to be baptized (Heinrich Euler, a Baptist friend from the youth movement, was visiting us and had agreed to perform the baptism at the spring in our woods). Unfortunately she could not be persuaded to wait, and as a result we were absent with the whole household on the morning of his arrival – a situation that I am sure did not help our relationship with him.

Another time the writer Eugen Jäckh, a friend of Christoph Friedrich Blumhardt,[1] came for a visit. Moved by the spirit he experienced among us, he said it reminded him of the parish of Bad Boll in Blumhardt's time, and mourned that it was "no longer like that there now." Eugen had compiled two volumes of writings by Blumhardt, and it was during this visit that Eberhard made plans to publish them.

Both father and son Blumhardt played an important role in our circle, and their expectation of God's kingdom gave us new enthusiasm every time we read their words. We were especially attentive to the elder Blumhardt's descriptions of healings in his parish – not only from physical sickness, but also from demonic possession – for we had similar experiences. But above all, our longing was directed toward the future kingdom, when love and justice will rule over the whole world, indeed, the whole universe.

The Swiss pastor Leonhard Ragaz, who gave up his professorship because of his love for the working class, also influenced us a great

---

[1] Christoph Friedrich Blumhardt (1842–1919), outspoken pastor, writer, and religious socialist; son of pastor and writer Johann Christoph Blumhardt (1805–1880).

deal at that time. We read many of his articles in our inner meetings and were deeply gripped and shaken by their message. I still vividly remember his words on faithfulness and on what it means to follow Christ. Unfortunately Leonhard was never able to visit us, but Eberhard corresponded with him regularly.

It was similar with Kees Boeke, a friend and fellow seeker in Holland. Though wealthy when they married, Kees and his wife Betty (formerly Cadbury, of British chocolate fame) had felt called to give their possessions to the poor and to live in community, and after World War I they had started a "brotherhood house" in Bilthoven.

I had met Kees during the winter of 1920–1921, when he came to Sannerz with several delegates of the Fellowship of Reconciliation for talks with us about the "new life." Others who took part were Oliver Dryer from England, John Nevin Sayre from America, and Henri Rosier from France; there may have been others too. These meetings were our first since the war with representatives of "enemy" nations, and they filled us with courage and hope for the future. Here were men who shared our dream of building up a new world—a new age in a new spirit of reconciliation.

Another important visit was that of Rudolf Koch. A famous graphic designer and calligrapher, Rudolf was also a man with a vision for the future, and he took an active part in the movements of the time. Just in the days he was staying with us, the house was full to overflowing with guests, and we decided it was finally time to write up a set of guidelines for visitors. Rudolf wrote these out in his bold, beautiful script, and we fixed the sheet to the dining room wall.

House rule or no, we tried to be as generous as possible. As a favorite rhyme of ours from those years went: "Ten were invited, but twenty came. Add water to the soup, and greet them all the same!" Speaking of food, our cooking was the simplest fare imaginable. I myself spent very little time in the kitchen because of the many guests, and most of the young women who came were either factory workers, typists, or teachers, or else members of well-to-do homes.

On top of that, it sometimes happened that the cook (though we did not have anyone who could really be called that!) was found sitting outside, painting or writing poetry while the potatoes boiled over, the wood fire went out, or the soup burned. Nobody worried about it too much; in fact, such things were usually laughed off:

> Cook, what have you for dinner tonight?
> Noodles again? Oh thunder and blight!
> Burned were they by roaring flame;
> Cook, tell us, is this not a shame?
> Noodles burned so crisp and black
> Are hardly fit for dog or cat.

Yes, we grown-ups did not lose too much sleep over these things – we had not exactly been spoiled during the previous years of war and revolution. I only found it hard at times on account of the children. In addition to our own, we had taken in several from extremely poor conditions, some of them no more than one or two years old, and not one of them was well nourished. Amazingly, some of our guests could not understand that these children needed better food than we adults. One asked me, "Why should the children have milk and eggs instead of herrings, beans, and dried peas as we grown-ups do? Don't we want to share *everything?*"

Sannerz, 1921. Standing (L to R): Bob Hettenhausen, Anke Schulz, Otto Salomon, Suse Hungar, Paul Hummel. Sitting (L to R): Emmy, Eberhard, Paul Oberländer, Else von Hollander, Eva Oehlke.

In the first year at Sannerz, aside from Eberhard and myself (and aside from our hundreds of guests), there were five others who belonged to our original circle: my sister Else, Otto Salomon, Eva Oehlke, Suse Hungar, and Gertrud Cordes. Together we were known, half jokingly, as "the holy seven." We were a fighting band, in the process of growth, and we talked over everything, worked out everything together. But we were not so close-knit as to have committed ourselves to each other for life, as members of our community do now.

Toward the end of 1921 our household grew rapidly, perhaps too rapidly. Of those who had been our guests and helpers during the summer, a considerable number – more than forty – stayed on to spend the winter with us. Because of dry weather and our lack of experience, the harvest was poor that year, but our publishing venture was doing well, and we used all the labor we could for that. Otto Salomon worked there, as did Fritz Schloss, Else Böhme (who came from the Furche Publishing House), Lotte Scriba, Hedwig Buxbaum, Eva Oehlke, and of course Else and Eberhard, who worked together primarily on the magazine *Das neue Werk*. All told, it was quite a crew working in the three front rooms of the ground floor. Nearly every day someone had to go to the printers in Schlüchtern (a walk of one-and-a-half hours) – we were so busy turning out new books and articles.

Meanwhile the farmwork was expanding too, and Eberhard invited an old friend to help us with it. When he arrived with his young wife, it turned out that though he was a very nice young man, a true idealist for our cause, he hardly knew anything about agriculture. First, he arranged for the villagers to remove our manure heap free of charge, because it was "such an eyesore." Naturally, the farmers in the village were delighted – though horrified at such ignorance. Then he fetched whole cartloads of beanpoles from a nearby forest, which belonged to the wealthy owner of a nearby castle, and proudly exclaimed, "We'll soon have the Baroness's whole forest down." If only he had remembered to plant the beans! Sometimes he would sit under the cow, with his big horn-rimmed glasses, trying to milk and compose poetry at the same time, to the great amusement

The five Arnold children with foster and orphan children at Sannerz, 1921.

of the villagers. Needless to say none of this made for much confidence in our farming methods.

Our educational work went better. Suse Hungar, the Salvation Army woman who had come with us from Berlin, was a trained teacher; so was Gertrud Dalgas (later Hüssy), who joined us in October 1921. Trudi, as she was called, had been a young teacher in Frankfurt and heard Eberhard speak in the adult education center *(Volksbildungsheim)* there, after which she attended our Whitsun conference, gave up her job, and came to work with us, full of energy and joy.

On the same day that Trudi arrived, my sister Moni joined us. She was working as a midwife in Halle at the time, and came at first simply because she "enjoyed our way of life." Soon she decided to stay for good. My eldest sister, Olga, and her adopted daughter, Ruth, who was seven years old, also lived with us during the summer of 1921. (Olga later moved on, but Ruth stayed for good.)

Here I want to tell about the wedding of Gertrud Cordes, a member of our circle and the daughter of a wealthy businessman, and Hermann Thoböll, a young medical doctor. The wedding was not at Sannerz, but Eberhard and I were invited to it, for we were friends of her parents and had often been guests at their country residence in the first years of our marriage.

Gertrud and Hermann wanted their marriage to be celebrated in the youth movement style; they did not want a "bourgeois" church wedding, a bridal veil, the traditional German myrtle wreath, and so on. Both sets of parents had everything prepared for an upper-middle-class wedding, however, and went ahead and bought a formal coat with tails for Hermann, and a long wedding gown for Gertrud. On the day of the wedding, the bridegroom appeared in a bright green tunic and shorts, and the bride in a simple white peasant dress with a garland of red clover in her hair. Instead of a procession, we followed the couple into a meadow, singing as we went, and sat down in a circle on the grass.

Eberhard was to perform the ceremony in the manner of the Quakers and of the youth movement. I no longer remember what he read or said, but it had something to do with love and faithfulness, and the meaning of the true church. Afterward Judge Thoböll, Hermann's father, demanded an official marriage certificate, so Heinrich Schultheis, a pastor and friend who attended the wedding with Eberhard and me, wrote one out.

Toward the end of 1921, so many people had come to live with us that we had to find an additional source of income. We thought of basketry, needlework, knitting – anything that might bring in something extra. As we considered our financial situation, it became apparent that not everyone saw the importance of our mission in the same light. For example, some wondered whether we should really be taking in needy children when we were barely able to support our own. But what else could we do? We had not asked for children – they had simply been brought to us!

During this time a second couple—Heinrich and Elisabeth Schultheis—came to us with their two small girls. Heinrich, a very outspoken pastor from Gelnhaar, had left his position because of his radical views; he no longer felt he could remain in the church. (Elisabeth, on the other hand, was middle-class in outlook and attempted to continue her accustomed lifestyle in our midst, which created more than a few tensions.)

After Christmas we concerned ourselves with the Letter to the Romans, especially chapter eight, where Paul writes about the victory of the Spirit. It was during our meetings on this theme that Otto Salomon, one of our original circle of seven, questioned our direction as a community for the first time. "How can we testify to Romans 8 if we still live in accordance with Romans 7?" he asked. Otto was referring to Paul's words, "I do not do what I want, but I do the very thing I hate…Who will deliver me from this body of death?" Someone explained that the eighth chapter does not say that we *are* delivered, but that we *can* be delivered. Otto was unconvinced.

After this there were many talks with him, individually and in the whole household. When Otto had joined the community a year-and-a-half earlier, he had said, "I am the camel. You can load on my back anything that is too much for you." But this initial faith and humility had long since gone. Now he said, "If I were to surrender completely to the call, I would not be able to produce art." And, "You have accepted so many worthless people into your midst that those who have something to give are beginning to stay away." Well, this no longer sounded like the man he was when he first came!

No wonder, then, that one day soon after this Otto came to tell us that he had joined Georg Flemmig's Young Men's Fellowship and wanted to leave our growing church community. Certainly there were other critical, even hostile voices making themselves heard already in those days, which we addressed in an article, "On the Criticism of Sannerz," in *Das neue Werk* of 1922. But Otto? His departure was an unexpected pain to all of us—the first person to leave our ranks! After he left, others in our circle also raised questions. Nevertheless, the good spirit led us together again and again.

Crisis

In the search for a new life, which was once so full of promise, a different influence began to make itself heard, also in print. It came especially from the ministers of various churches. Their motto was: "Let the people with the new vision return to the old ways of life, and let their light shine there." Through this the impetus of the movement came to a halt for many young people.

The Whitsun Conference of 1922 took place not in Sannerz but in Wallroth, in the Rhön hills, and the new "back-to-the-old" movement invited speakers like Wilhelm Stählin. The topics in themselves were an indication of a different direction: "Fanaticism and salvation in the youth movement," "Sannerz (fantasy, utopia) versus Habertshof (reality)." This latter title reflected the changes at the Habertshof, where the idea of taking the new vision back to the old life had taken root among many, especially through the influence of Emil Blum, a former Swiss pastor. Eberhard spoke, too, however. Among other things he talked about the "funeral" of the youth movement, and this caused great offense.

We continued to have many guests, including those who had attended the conference, and in our household there were many long evening discussions about the two directions in our movement. People took their stand on one side or the other. The fight had begun within our own ranks! Meanwhile our work continued in the publishing house and on the farm, though certainly interrupted by frequent talks.

In summer 1922 our family was invited to spend the month of July with the Boekes at Bilthoven, in Holland. Already that spring, Kees had given us money toward the purchase of a mill, as the house in Sannerz had become too small for the increasing number of people, and it did not seem worthwhile enlarging a building which, after all, was only rented.

The farmers in Sannerz had up to now rented us their poorest and stoniest fields, one reason being that we were "so many people" and therefore "well able" to pick the stones. I'm sure they also saw that we were not good farmers, and kept the best land for themselves. The fields that belonged to the mill were much better, on the other hand, and set in a most romantic spot, which made the idea very attractive. Besides, the publishing work could not support all sixty of us. To live and work more closely with nature – to experience the seasons of sowing and harvesting – surely this was a solution. But as the next months unfolded, it became clear that nothing would ever come of the idea.

As I mentioned, our whole family, including Else, had been invited to spend July in Bilthoven, and the community decided that we should accept; Eberhard and I were rather run down after the first two years in Sannerz, and the children's health was not much better as a result of post-war malnutrition. There had been increasing unrest in the community over the previous months, but we agreed to the trip and put our hope in the good spirit to overcome all difficulties and differences. We also trusted those who had fought and suffered through so much with us. Surely they still had faith in the future kingdom, which we did not think was far away! This vision lived in us.

In Holland we were welcomed warmly and looked after with great love. There was a lively, anti-militaristic spirit among the people in the Boekes' group, and every Saturday as many of them as possible marched in front of the town hall in Amsterdam, singing Kees's song, "No, no, we have done with fighting," in various languages.

On August 2, 1922, the eighth anniversary of the outbreak of the war, a big crowd of war resisters from Bilthoven and other places marched through Amsterdam with stuffed horses and peace flags with the inscription, "No More War." We also took part, of course, singing, "Long, long enough have Christian men borne arms against their brother," and other songs by Kees Boeke, all in Dutch. As the military columns marched past the Brotherhood House in Bilthoven, everyone opened the windows and shouted, *"Nooit meer oorlog!"* "No more war!"

Kees and Betty had a similar attitude with regard to money: they wouldn't even touch it. When they crossed a toll bridge, they gave eggs or something else. Neither did they believe in paying taxes, or obeying police officers, and they were put in prison many times because of this. One time Kees just lay flat on the ground and had to be bodily carried off. Their furniture and other possessions went up for auction over and over again, but each time their friends and wealthy relatives refurnished their home. And so the cycle repeated itself.

In other respects, too, the Bilthoven group was very radical. Every guest or helper could take part in their meetings, and every voice carried equal weight. As Kees expressed it, every person carries a light within, and the good spirit can move and speak through him. In this sense, everyone was allowed to voice his or her opinion on any practical question that arose. We took part in such meetings on a number of occasions, and they seemed rather chaotic to us. What we missed (and we expressed this) was the atmosphere of Christ, in whose spirit freedom is joined with reverence for a greater uniting power. In any case, Kees and Betty impressed us: they were an honest and forthright couple–people who put their convictions into action–and there was much we could learn from them.

While we were in Holland, letters came from home about the situation there, which sounded more and more disquieting. For one thing, financial worries had increased; inflation was soaring, loans (some from friends, and one from a bank) were being recalled, and we were suddenly faced with debts we had thought we had months to repay. Then Eberhard was asked to return home. In actual fact, as it was impossible to raise money in Germany, we felt it was providential that we were in Holland, and were confident that what was needed would be given to us there. Eberhard wrote home to say that he would be back before payment was due; that is, in two weeks if not sooner.

In spite of this, the unrest at home, as conveyed to us in letters from Sannerz, grew even greater. I was ready to travel with the children if need be, but Eberhard wanted to stay: during a long walk across the heath, he had received the inner certainty that he should not allow himself to be shaken out of his inner calm, but should complete his tasks in Holland as previously agreed, and be home by the time the payment on the bank loan was due. When we discussed the situation with Else, we came to the same conclusion. We felt a strong inner assurance that God would show us the way, if only we let him. Here I want to share lines from a letter Eberhard wrote to my sister Monika, just in those days:

> Take courage! We must no longer see what is small! The great must take hold of us in such a way that it also penetrates and transforms the small. I have courage and joy for our life again in the certainty, of course, that it will cost a great and glorious struggle. The Spirit will conquer the flesh! The Spirit is the stronger! He overwhelms me, you, one after the other. This Spirit is goodness, independence, and mobility.
>
> Our life will not become narrower, but broader; not more limited, but more boundless; not more regulated, but more abundant; not more pedantic, but more bounteous; not more sober, but more enthusiastic; not more faint-hearted, but more daring; not worse and more human, but filled with God and ever better; not sadder, but happier; not more incapable, but more creative. All this is Jesus and his spirit of freedom! He is coming to us. Therefore let us not grieve about anything, but forgive everyone, just as we must be forgiven everything, and go into the future radiant with joy. Stay and wait until you are clothed with power from on high.

Soon the letters from home began speaking of our "gross lack of responsibility;" we even found out that those who had stayed at Sannerz asked the Brotherhood House in Bilthoven to send whatever money they wanted to give us directly to their address, rather than give it to us. (The Boekes did not heed this advice.)

Our departure from Holland came quickly. On our last evening a lady handed us an envelope containing Dutch guilders. When Eberhard went to the bank in the morning, he received in German currency the exact amount owed by our publishing house to the bank on that very date. For once the inflation had worked to our advantage! Eberhard called home to share the good news, but was met with the reply, "It is too late; the publishing house is already being liquidated!"

After this we traveled home, spending a night in Frankfurt and arriving at Sannerz the next day. Suse, Moni, and Trudi met us at the station in Schlüchtern. Suse looked petrified and said only that she was not to tell us anything. At home we had an icy reception and watery soup. A small cake had been baked for the children, however.

After dinner we were invited to a meeting; everyone sat in a circle on the floor of the dining room, the largest room in the house. The windows were wide open, and sitting on the sills, or looking in from outside, were students and others from a conference that was meeting in Schlüchtern that same day. (Eberhard had been scheduled to give the opening address, and several of the participants had come over, wanting to see something of Sannerz.)

Inside the room, a struggle erupted and raged as the conflict that had been slowly brewing over the previous months finally came to a head. On the one side were those of us who felt we must leave the old ways for once and for all if we were going to build up something truly new; on the other were those who advised us to give up our "idealism." It was said that faith and economic matters didn't belong together, whereas we felt that faith must penetrate and direct everything, including financial matters. Max Wolf had put it best in a publishing house meeting just days before: "What separates Eberhard Arnold from the rest of us is his conviction that faith must determine *all* relationships, including financial ones."

Finally, it was said that our "open door" was nothing but a great lie – that we had held meetings of both an inner and practical nature at which not everybody was present. It was true; we had sometimes gathered late in the day, when most people were already in bed, to discuss the various challenges and problems our numerous guests brought with them, and to try to find a way of moving ahead. But mostly we had met this way simply to gather inward strength for the next stretch of the way.

It was not an easy meeting, to be sure. But the discussions that followed were even more difficult, and there was a palpable atmosphere of darkness and hostility in the room. When Eberhard stated that we were not willing to change the direction, but that we were ready to continue living with them in a modest, unassuming manner, if someone else would agree to take over the leadership, the upheaval knew no bounds. One after the other stood up and declared his intention to leave Sannerz. There must have been about forty in all. We could hardly comprehend all this, as we had gone through so much with many of them. What had happened during our absence of four weeks? It was inconceivable!

At the end, when the person in charge of the meeting asked who still intended to stay, there were just seven, the smallest possible

Eberhard and Emmy, 1922.

number to enable us to continue as a legally incorporated body. Had there been fewer, Sannerz would have been automatically dissolved, and the money for the mill, as well as all the inventory, would have been distributed among those who were currently living in the house.

Our business manager at the time, a former bank clerk named Kurt Harder, was among those who wanted to leave. Apart from him, the executive council consisted of Heinrich Schultheis (who had also decided to go), Eberhard, and myself. Because no more than two signatures were required for the transaction of business, anything could be done without Eberhard and myself, and it was. Furniture, farm implements – even our cows and other animals – were sold off. We city folk were unable to look after them properly, it was said. Canning jars were bought so that those moving away could take along as much of the plentiful fruit and vegetables as possible. Firewood we had stacked up for winter was burned in the stoves with the windows wide open, though it was only early September. People even used the money earmarked for the mill to purchase overcoats, shirts, and other clothing items, and urged us to do the same. Their rage exceeded all bounds when we refused to accept a share of it.

But the sum had been given for a common cause; Kees had never intended for it to be divided among individuals.

Now accusations of fraud were hurled at us from all sides, and the situation became almost unbearable. Naturally those who had turned against the community could not leave until they found another livelihood elsewhere, and the days seemed to drag. The Schultheises, together with several others, looked into other possibilities for community living; after a while they found a suitable place in a former children's home at Gelnhausen. But their community only survived for a few months, and no wonder–there was nothing to hold them together except their protest against our way.

In the meantime our little group had taken on cooking for the whole household. I did most of it, but as I was not used to the thin, green soups we ate so often in those years, I tried to prepare more nourishing food, though in smaller amounts. The others thought we were trying to starve them. Eberhard immediately advised me to increase the quantities, which I did. It meant starting to cook again right after each meal, but what else could we do? More than ever we felt the importance of acting in accordance with the words of Jesus in the Sermon on the Mount–of going the second mile.

Our situation–having no community but living together in the same house–became more and more intolerable as the days went by. Among those staying with us were several young women who had not come to us on account of any inward urge, but who simply needed a place to stay. One had been entrusted to our care by the welfare office; another had come to have her baby in a safe place. Both spread rumors around the house, which certainly did not make life any easier.

One bright spot in those dreary days was the visit of Ernst Ferdinand Klein, an uncle with whom Eberhard had spent the summer vacation of 1899, who had been instrumental in his conversion that same year. Onkel Ernst came to us from Berlin with his wife Lisbeth to "experience the spirit of Sannerz," and we were anxious as to what he would find. At first he did not take sides, and in his loving way tried to bring about reconciliation. When that didn't work, he went throughout the house each day, knocking at every door and inviting everyone to morning devotions! Amazingly, they all came: nobody was able to resist such a lovable man. And it did help to make the situation more bearable.

Although there were very likable people among those planning to leave – people who had been deeply moved and inspired for community at one time – a spirit of hatred now came from them. How could we be so foolish, so stubbornly determined to continue on the way we had recognized, they wondered? But we had never considered Sannerz a mere experiment, as apparently they had, an experiment for which, they said, "our generation is too weak, too human, too selfish." To us, it was a matter of a calling.

Here I should mention the liquidation of the Neuwerk Publishing House. First the partners and shareholders met to officially wind up the publishing work, which, in their opinion, had not been run in a businesslike manner. Then the books were divided up: those leaving us planned to start an imprint of their own, and wanted to take the books most suitable for this, including *Junge Saat,* both Blumhardt volumes, our Georg Flemmig titles, and others, above all the magazine *Das neue Werk.* We were heartbroken. It was an act of kindness on the part of our old friend Otto Herpel, who died soon afterward, to leave the Zinzendorf volume with us. He said, "We respect Eberhard's faith, even though we cannot share it." Yes, even he was of the opinion that spiritual and temporal matters ought not to be mixed.

At the end of the meeting a vote was taken to determine whether all agreed to proceed with the liquidation. It seemed there was a unanimous yes – until Eberhard stood up and said, "Unanimous with the exception of one voice! I am not in agreement. Please record this in the minutes!"

Finally, in October, the last of our former household members left, and Sannerz was quiet. Yet there was still a great obstacle to overcome. Before leaving, our "friends" had gone to the government housing office, declaring that the house was soon going to be empty, and that rooms would be available for people who needed a place to live. (There were still many homeless people, even four years after the end of the war.)

We were summoned to appear before the local court in Schlüchtern. The plaintiffs had hired a sharp lawyer, who proceeded to state their case very aggressively, and the judge had a plan of the whole house, showing the layout of the rooms. Eberhard and I were quite alone. We made it clear that the work of the community had not been closed down, nor had its social work been discontinued; only a certain number of people were leaving. We also reminded the court that if it was really a lack of housing for homeless citizens that was at stake, there was always the castle in nearby Ramholz, which belonged to local nobility and stood empty almost the whole year round. Finally the judge stated his decision: the court recognized that the law was on our side, and we were thus permitted to continue using the house at Sannerz for our needs and for the purposes of our work.

When we came home, there was great rejoicing. Now, after all the hardships and the disillusionment of the past months, after so many beloved friends who had originally shared our enthusiasm for a new way had left us, we could once again rebuild. And we were determined to do this, with every ounce of energy we had. It was not so, as some might think, that the "weaker" or "worse" ones had left, and the "better" or "stronger" ones remained. We did not feel that way at all. We were very much aware of our own failings and inadequacies for the task at hand. Yet in spite of our limitations we *had* to go on. Many years later, just two months before he died in November 1935, Eberhard said of this time:

> When the call first came to us, we felt that the spirit of Christ had charged us to live in full community, in communal solidarity, with an open door and a loving heart for all people. It was the word of Jesus Christ, the reality of his life and his spirit that gave us the strength to start out on this way and to keep going though our steps were small and feeble. We had traveled only a short distance on this way when times came upon us that put this power to the test, times of trial and hostility, when friends we had grown to love deeply suddenly reversed their position and became enemies because they had turned from freedom and unity and wanted to return to ordinary middle-class life, to a "normal, private life" and their own pocketbook. Thus the movement was led into bondage again through the influence of capitalism and its professional and business life.

Yet even though most of our friends left us and whole groups deserted the flag of unity and freedom, though well-meaning people earnestly warned us that this way would lead to a lonely and ineffectual end, we were not dissuaded. With our own children and those we had adopted, we had to push through toward the goal.

It was around this time that Eberhard and Else traveled to Berlin to discuss the continuation of our publishing work; they brought back with them Hans Grimm, a motherless ten-year-old. During these same days we received a telegram regarding our sister Olga, asking us if she could come to Sannerz. Olga had contracted tuberculosis a year-and-a-half earlier and had stayed with us during the summer of 1921, together with her adopted daughter Ruth; now it seemed she was in the last stages of her illness.

Moni and I immediately traveled to Lippe (Olga's home) and found her very ill. She told us how hard the previous months had been for her, and what a struggle she had been through when she realized how little time she had left. But she had fought through her depression, and now she was filled with a joyful anticipation of eternity. She longed to see the "city of golden streets," to meet Jesus, the apostles, her parents, and other loved ones who had died.

It was November, and Olga was sad that she would never experience spring again – the earthly spring with its violets and cowslips, and other wild flowers. But how eagerly she looked forward to the eternal spring! We were deeply moved by her attitude of faith, and brought

Emmy's sister Olga von Hollander (1882–1922).

her home. Little Ruth traveled with us; from then on she was part of our family for good.

At Sannerz we put Olga in a relatively large room, with two big windows facing south. Still, heating was quite a problem. As I said earlier, all of our firewood had been recklessly burned, and because we had no money to buy more, we had to collect what we could from the Albing Mountain. Every day as many of us as possible went out to collect fuel for all the stoves—and there were many of them. Even the children helped—as with other chores, they joined us eagerly and with enthusiasm.

The wood was not good—in fact, it was mostly green—and the smoky fires it made were no help for Olga's lungs. Her coughing attacks and breathing difficulties were terrible to watch. Moni and I would have preferred to have her stay in the hospital in Schlüchtern, where conditions were better, but Olga would have none of it. She wanted to die "at home," surrounded by her sisters and our little circle of fellow believers.

The last few weeks with Olga were a great challenge to us all. So close to death she was, and yet so close to the life that lasts eternally! Mr. Orth, the senior pastor of Schlüchtern who visited her during her last days, said, "For her, passing into the other world is like stepping from one room into the other."

Sometimes we sat at her bedside in small groups—Else, Moni, Trudi, Hugga (Suse Hungar), and Eberhard and I—singing old and new Advent songs. At other times one of us sat alone with her, listening to her as she spoke of her longing for redemption from suffering and her expectation of glory. Because of the danger of infection, little Ruth was allowed to visit her only once a day. When she came, Olga encouraged her in her childlike way, expressing her hope that one day Ruth would find the way to Christ.

On Olga's last night, the night of December 1, I went to bed with a cold and a fever. Ruth and Emy-Margret were in the room next to mine, Olga in the room directly above. Suddenly both girls came in and wanted to talk with me. While we were still talking, I heard the door above me being locked. I knew, even before my sisters could tell me, that Olga had died.

Eberhard had not been home for several days; he was in Sonnefeld at the time, meeting with Hans Klassen and his group of inspired young Baptists—the group that later started the settlement of the so-called Neu-Sonnefeld Youth. We sent a telegram, and he returned home quickly.

Two days after Olga's death we celebrated the first Sunday of Advent. The songs we sang reflected our experience, especially the one, "How shall I fitly meet thee?" which we sang with great emotion as we thought of our dear sister lying in her room. Otto Salomon's song, "Lo, a light is in the East" is another I remember singing at the time. The funeral, which took place in Ramholz, was held the following day. We took the coffin to the cemetery on a simply decorated farm wagon.

We missed Olga, but her death held no terror for us. Was it not a going home to Christ, and did it not carry within it the power of resurrection? Dying was a stark reminder of the crisis we had just been through as a community: the powers of death had tried to destroy a movement that had been awakened to life, and had almost conquered it. Yet out of this very struggle, painful as it was, new hope and strength had arisen like a breath of spring. More than ever we felt ready to defend the cause at all costs.

6

A New Start

After the crisis of 1922 we would have liked to have some time to ourselves, but we were not left alone. Many people came out of curiosity, wanting to know how things were going in Sannerz, and there continued to be plenty of criticism regarding all that had happened. This was true even far from home. Earlier, when we had attended conferences, people were full of enthusiasm for what they knew of our life; now, when they found out where we were from, they often moved quickly away. Comments like, "Sannerz is one big lie," or "Sannerz is nothing but an idealist utopia" were spread far and wide and accepted as fact. We could not disprove anything with words; our only answer was to invite our detractors to come and see our life for themselves before judging it. Looking back, I find it a miracle that we were able to continue in spite of it all.

Among those who lived with us in the house at the time were several unwed expectant mothers, most of them needy, who had somehow heard about us. One of them, Friedel, had first stayed at our home in Berlin and in 1920 we had taken her in a second time after she completed a prison term for robbing a department store. Now she showed up a third time, expecting a baby and needing a place to live. Unfortunately the villagers in our mainly Catholic district misunderstood our hospitality in cases like this, and it did not help our already questionable reputation.

We have often been asked about our attitude to this sort of outreach in those early years. Simply put, we made an effort to take in all who came to us for help. Moni was a trained midwife and therefore able to provide medical assistance, and we all supported her. It was not a matter of social work; it was a deed of love.

As for the fruits of our efforts, there were practically none, other than disappointments. Having regained their strength among us (at no cost to themselves, of course) our mothers usually disappeared, with or without baby. Was that to stop us from doing the work of love? The question came up again and again, in part because of our image as a community. But we rejected it as a temptation, as cowardice. Yes, there was little thankfulness for the pains we took, but it was not for the sake of thanks that we did it.

Children continued to be brought to us; visitors came and went – some seeking, some merely curious. Karl Keiderling (Roland, as we called him then) came just in time to help us get the last potatoes out of the ground. He also helped us gather firewood from the forest, a daily necessity. At Christmas, Agnes, a youth leader, came for a time with a small group of girls. It wasn't an easy visit, for we had the feeling they wanted to observe us rather than to experience something with us. In general, everything went at a slower pace, and we found more time to gather inwardly and re-find our bearings. Eberhard's poem, "I start again anew to live," which was put to music by our friend Walther Böhme, expresses the mood we felt very well.

In 1923 the publishing house was newly established from the ground up as the *Eberhard Arnold Verlag;* those who had left us had taken the well-known Neuwerk name and logo away with them. Of the Neuwerk-period books, we kept only Otto Herpel's *Zinzendorf,* two dramas that Otto Salomon had brought with him, Goldstein's book on race, and the little anthology of legends. Tolstoy's letters and Emil Engelhardt's book on love and marriage were being printed at the time.

We had few resources, but Kees Boeke had told us to keep the rest of the money meant for the mill after the expenses had been covered for those who had left, so at least we had something. It was also at this time that, through our connections with the Baptist Youth, we took over joint publication of the magazine *Die Wegwarte* with them.

Most gratifying of all, a relationship developed with the Hochweg Publishing House in Berlin, which finally made it possible to pursue Eberhard's dream of a series of *Quellen* ("source books") on various religious currents – and the notable men and women in them – throughout history.

As each new volume came into being, it was an enrichment for all of us to share in the witness of its subject. While sorting potatoes in the cellar, or making preserves, we read parts of the manuscript aloud, and everyone took a lively interest. The authors of several of the *Quellen* volumes came to visit us, which made it possible for us to acquaint ourselves more intimately with their work: Alexander Beyer, author of the volume on Francis of Assisi; Karl Justus Obenauer, author of *Novalis;* Hermann Ulrich, who edited the *Diaries of Kierkegaard;* and Alfred Wiesenhuetter, editor of *Jakob Böhme.* Through this we gained a deeper understanding of the historical context of these books. In the case of Eberhard's book *The Early Christians,* we all participated in the compiling process by selecting passages from the materials he shared with us. (Two "source books" that were planned but unfortunately never finished were Eberhard's book on the nonresistant Anabaptists of the sixteenth century, and Theo Spira's volume on George Fox).

Because I had been interested in religious songs and hymns since my early youth and had also selected most of the songs we sang together, I was asked to make a collection of Zinzendorf's songs in their original form from the Moravian archives in Herrnhut. They were to be appended to Otto Herpel's volume on Zinzendorf. I enjoyed this work very much. I also compiled and edited the book *Sonnenlieder* (Songs of the Sun), our first collection for communal singing. It was a lot of work, but a project that brought me great joy.

The trips we made to the printer in the romantic old city of Würzburg were most memorable and enjoyable. While Eberhard and Else went to the printers, I went shopping; afterward we would spend several hours in the Café Zeissner reading proofs together. It was wonderful!

One thing that occupied us anew in 1923 – though it was important to us from the beginning of our life together – was the building up of our children's community. The older children, Emy-Margret, Hardy, and Heinrich, had not remained untouched by the turmoil of the year before, and they needed our love and attention. They were aware of the conflicting spirits that had shaken the house, and of the hatred that had come to expression in remarks like, "Sannerz is just a big lie. It ought to be destroyed, lock, stock, and barrel." They knew too, how their father had been personally slandered and attacked.

Of course, our children's education was not limited to school-work, but included other activities. In summer, for instance, there were the glorious berry-picking excursions we made for days on end, gathering in the harvest given by God by day, and at evening performing simple dramas like "The Water of Life" for the farmers in whose barns we found a place to sleep.

Standing under the *Dorflinde*—the old linden in the center of each village—we would sing the old folk songs, accompanied by violins and guitars. In return, the peasants would treat us to bread, sausage, and eggs. After two or three days a wagon came from home to bring back the buckets full of the berries "God had given us without our sowing," as Eberhard always said. The friendship of the peasants, the working and playing and singing together with our children—all this was sheer happiness! And the harvest, which often amounted to over a hundred pounds, was something we depended on.

By now there were fifteen or more children at Sannerz, including our own five. These were the years of the "Sun Troop," a small group started by our son Heinrich and his classmates, Sophie and Luise, all three of whom felt a strong urge to share their faith with other children in the village. Because the oldest of these children was no more than eleven, it was tempting at times to hold them back until they could become more mature. Yet Eberhard and I could not help rejoicing in their childlike enthusiasm, which made them value their hearts' experience above their homework, their chores, and every-thing else. It reminded us of the spirit that must have animated the Children's Crusades, and the children's revival at the time of Zinzendorf.

Nearly all the children of Heinrich's age joined the Sun Troop. Carrying their red banner, they would walk to a quiet meadow or a place in the woods where they held their meetings, talking, singing, or reading together. Sometimes it was the Bible, or a legend; at others they read from the mystic Meister Eckhart, whose writings Heinrich loved especially. They had their own campfires and their own songs,

(L to R) Luise Kolb, Heinrich Arnold, and Sophie Schwing at Sannerz, mid 1920s.

and they did not like it when someone eavesdropped, though they did invite this or that one to a meeting on occasion. Heinrich put his zeal into words in a childlike song he wrote at the time:

> We would a fire kindle
> Eagerly, with great joy.
> We would a song be singing
> That makes our hearts rejoice.
> Fire toward Christ shall blazing start,
> To all shall bring a new loving heart,
> Shall brightly shine afar.

A song written by Emy-Margret at the time of the 1922 crisis was another favorite:

> Now when our brothers prepare for battle,
> And in their breasts a fire is kindled,
> They march through town and countryside
> With courage and victorious cries.
>
> They wander with an impulse holy
> To sow the seeds of love to brothers.

They fight against all war and strife,
They fight against all sinfulness.

With truly joyful hearts they're marching,
With really clear and radiant sun-hearts,
And Jesus Christ before them goes,
And after him run all who can.

Marcel Woitzschach, a coffeehouse musician who was living with us at the time, wrote a tune for this poem. He was drawn to our life of brotherhood, but disillusioned by our struggles too, and later he left. Sad to say, we never heard from him again.

As our school grew, so did our need for teachers. Trudi Dalgas and Suse Hungar had been with us since 1921; later Ludwig Wedel came to help for a while. He was influenced by eastern mysticism, and after he left us he went to India, where he lived in an ashram for many years. Anneliese Dittrich, a teacher from Bremen, joined us some time later and taught in our school too.

In 1923 Georg Barth visited us for the first time. Trained in industrial arts but strongly influenced by the mystics and by the contemporary youth movement, he was a real enrichment to our small group. Previously Georg had worked in a home for delinquent boys; now he agreed to teach our children handicrafts and oversee their involvement in the practical work. In 1925 he came to stay.

The arrival of Adolf and Martha Braun and their two daughters, Elfriede and Gertrud, was a high point of 1924. They were the first family to join us since the crisis of 1922. Adolf had first become aware of us by reading Eberhard's book *War: A Call to the Inner Land* while lying in an army hospital in Constantinople during World War I. After the war, back in Germany, he had attended public lectures where Eberhard had spoken, and visited us a number of times. Now he and Martha had decided to come for good; they had sold their house in Nordhausen, and bought train tickets to Schlüchtern.

On the day of the Braun's arrival, full of joy and anticipation, we went to meet them at the station, our farm wagon decorated with greenery and flowers, and the older children carrying torches. Young men and women had joined us before, and we were grateful for each

A farm wagon like this one (1933, with Emmy at the reins) greeted the Brauns on their arrival at Sannerz in 1924.

one. But here, at long last, was another *family* who dared to join our adventure! Two others came from the Braun's church: Rose Meyer (later Kaiser), and a few weeks later, Lotte Henze.

At Sannerz the Brauns told us that on their way, at the railroad station in Kassel, "friends" who had left us in 1922 had tried to dissuade them from coming. That made us even more grateful to have them among us, and to know that they could have our full trust.

While Martha was a little "bourgeois" at first, Adolf soon felt at home. True to the youth movement ideal of simplicity, he wanted nothing but the plainest, and though he had brought a huge vanload of furniture with him, he wanted to keep only a minimum. In his opinion, a few simple chairs and a box for a table were ample. Adolf's advice in several difficult financial situations was also a great help, as was his courage in asking for extensions on loans and postponement of bills. It was not long before we asked him to join the executive council of our legal society.

Eberhard and I, Trudi and Else, and now Adolf were members of this council; I still remember how, after taking care of business in Schlüchtern or Fulda, the five of us would take time to relax in a café together. Especially when we had been dealing with a financial problem, those hours of fellowship brought us close.

Money was not our main worry in those days however, particularly in light of the inner struggles we experienced after 1922. People came to us tormented – perhaps even possessed – by demonic powers, and often it seemed that the more powerfully the Holy Spirit worked in our midst, the harder their struggle became. Some were freed from the darkness that beset them in a quiet, unobtrusive way. But there were two (one a guest, the second a member of our household) who were enslaved by unclean spirits, and their struggle was much more difficult. Eberhard and I and several others took an active part in the fight against these powers.

We were concerned not only with the burdened souls themselves, for we felt we were involved in a battle of spirits – good against evil. As the apostle Paul wrote: "We are not contending against flesh and blood, but against principalities and powers, against the world rulers of this present darkness, against spiritual hosts of wickedness in the heavenly places."

Oswald, a big, brawny man who wore little clothing, appeared suddenly one day, his long hair tied with a pink ribbon. At first we did not make much of his odd ways, but when he suddenly disrobed completely during a communal midday meal, saying, "To the pure everything is pure," we knew we were dealing with something more than eccentricity, and sent him from the room.

Later, we confronted Oswald about his behavior and became more fully aware what a miserable and tortured man he was. When Eberhard asked him whether he wanted to be freed from the impure spirits that so obviously bound him, he retorted with a diabolical grin, "You can't do it!" Eberhard held firm: "But the church can." At this Oswald ran out of the room, screaming, "I am afraid; this has to do with death and the devil. This means I have to die!" Oswald ran so fast that no one could catch up with him; we never heard of him again.

Our struggle with sixteen-year-old Lotte Henze was quite different, and far more intense. From the beginning, Lotte often wore a peculiar expression, and it was obvious that there was something unusual about her. Certainly, there were times when she looked quite normal, but at others there was a tormented, almost evil, look on her face.

One day Lotte would respond positively to our life, telling us openly about her difficult childhood and asking searching questions that went far beyond her age; the next she would act quite differently, uttering ugly and hateful words. Eberhard was troubled about her, and we assigned her to help me in the work, so that I could support her in difficult moments.

One day Lotte begged to be baptized. All of us felt this would help her, and we soon began to hold meetings to prepare for baptism. Our son Heinrich took part, too, as did Karl Keiderling, who had just returned after a time of absence from the community. In the end the meetings only resulted in greater internal conflicts for Lotte, and we decided to postpone the actual baptism, also for Heinrich and Karl. Here I will let Eberhard's words (from a letter to a group of Christian publishers in April 1926) speak for themselves:

> We have been through rough times this winter. One struggle was due to our lack of finances…and this tough fight alone could have consumed all our strength…
>
> The other was considerably more difficult, more fateful. I can only indicate its nature in broad strokes; the details cannot be told here. We found ourselves in a spiritual struggle against dark powers which developed a force such as we had never known before…We had come face to face with demonic powers before, and seen what power they can have over people. But never had we come across it in such a frightening way as we did this winter. We had to be right there day and night until, after weeks of wrestling, the strength of the hostile power was broken.
>
> It was a help to our small community that we had the example of the early Christians to reveal the power which conquers demons. The victory given Johann Christoph Blumhardt in 1843 after his fight against demonic powers in his parish at Möttlingen was also an encouragement to us. The sinister manifestations and terrifying blasphemies, the storming and raving, the possession of the tormented person by the evil power, the attack on the faith of the believers – all this can be broken only by the name of Jesus Christ, by witnessing to his life, from the virgin birth to his words and deeds, his crucifixion, and his resurrection.

Members of Sannerz at a conference in Eisenach, 1925. Seated, center (L to R): Eberhard, daughter Emy-Margret, Getrud Dalgas, and Monika von Hollander (with guitar).

Only by the power and authority of the Holy Spirit can evil powers be broken; an individual can do nothing. The church alone is empowered to command them, no matter how small a handful of devoted believers represents it. When this authority is given, the demonic powers become anxious and fearful, and the possessed person may express this by physical collapse or by fleeing and hiding. The important thing, then, is to hold on, to believe in Christ, and to banish the evil power completely through him until the possessed person is freed and can herself call upon Christ.

God gave us this victory–it was a memorable New Year's Eve–and through this, some among us found a new faith (and a new awareness of their own human smallness) such as they never had before. It became clear that the main thing was not the individual and his or her salvation, but the struggle for supremacy between two spiritual forces. It was a conflict between God and Satan–between the only good power, the power of the Holy Spirit, and the evil forces of the demons. And it made us more certain than ever that the kingdom of God is *power*.

The struggles were drawn out over a period of weeks and often went on at night, so that afterward we were exhausted. Then, in the months that followed (and they were almost more difficult) the person who had undergone such unspeakable torment had to be guided back to faith...for in spite of all that had happened, this was not yet assured. Then there were doubts and misgivings among those who had held on to faith most courageously in the hardest days of the fight, because the person in question suffered several relapses...Regretfully, our attention became focused too much on this person in the end, and this distracted us from our love for God.

Now our little community needs to be strengthened once more in hours of quiet...so that Christ may purify us and prepare us. We still stand in the midst of a struggle, but it is one of becoming. We stand at the beginning of a new time.

We ask you from our hearts to have patience with us in this situation and, above all, to continue supporting us through your practical help and your prayers. May God fan the flames of the decisive struggle in his church everywhere, and lead it to victory.

Your brother, Eberhard Arnold

P. S. You will realize that this information is strictly confidential, and that I wrote it all only because of my trust in your friendship. As much as possible, things of this nature should be kept quiet.

Yes, those days of intense struggle repeatedly reminded us of Blumhardt's fight; and we believed that Lotte would become a part of our life for good, in the same way that the tormented Gottliebin had become part of Blumhardt's household in his day. This was not given, however. Lotte's struggles did not recur, at least not while she stayed with us, but after a year or so she left us. Later she returned from time to time to visit us, once with a child, and then in the early 1930s we heard that the Gestapo had arrested her on account of her involvement with the Communists, and sent her to a concentration camp. That was the last we heard of her.

The Rhön Bruderhof

Our door remained open for entering and for leaving, and many people came and went. All kinds of people came looking for refuge with us. One young visitor had run away from her husband and sought shelter with us; another, wanted by the police, suddenly vanished behind a cupboard during one of our communal meals: he had looked out the window and seen them approaching. A young girl came all the way from Berlin because of an unhappy love affair her father had put an end to. There were many reasons people showed up at Sannerz—and they were not always of the deepest nature.

In the mid-1920s, several young men joined us: among them Alfred Gneiting, Arno Martin, Hans Zumpe, Fritz Kleiner, and Kurt Zimmermann. All of these stayed with us for good. Others helped out for a time but got tired of the hardships of our life. Tramps—"brothers of the road," as we called them—often turned up too. Unemployment was widespread in Germany for years after the war, and many were forced into a life on the road, hunting for a day's work wherever they could find it.

As our household grew to about fifty, Sannerz became too small, and we were forced to start looking for a new property, even though we had no money. Before long we heard of the Sparhof, a large farm a few miles away. It was an isolated spot with rocky soil, and the local peasants did not have a very good reputation, but that did not frighten us. Hadn't we always sought out the poor?

The Sparhof consisted of seven farmsteads, the largest of which—the Hansehof—was seventy-five acres. Ownership had changed hands many times because of debts and deaths, and the buildings were dilapidated and the fields neglected. On top of this there were strings attached—the couple who lived on the farm had the right to stay on

The "Hansehof" as it appeared in 1926, the year it was purchased by the household at Sannerz and renamed the Rhön Bruderhof.

the property until their death. Yet it was the only place we found that seemed to offer any possibilities, and the asking price was favorable: 26,000 marks.

Run down as it was, the farmstead was not far from Sannerz, which was an important point in its favor. We had no idea where would we find the 10,000 marks needed for the down payment, or how we could raise the funds needed to rebuild and enlarge the main house, which was completely uninhabitable. But we were eager to build a "monument" to communal life, as Eberhard expressed it, and not afraid of work. If the step was right, it must be taken, and taken in faith. We decided to buy the place.

In the fall of 1926 the community sent Eberhard and me to speak with the owners; next we traveled to Fulda, hoping it would be possible to sign the contract. Else and I sat in the Café Hesse waiting for Eberhard to return from the notary's office. When he came to fetch us to sign our names, I wavered, wondering aloud how we could possibly sign without having a penny of the 10,000 marks we would need as down payment within ten days. Naturally we had told a number of friends our plans, and we hoped for a gift here or there, but we knew of no one who might give us such a sum. Yet Eberhard was adamant: "This is a step in faith!"

Our payment day grew closer, and still there was no money. Then, on the last day before the money was due, a friend, the Prince of Schönburg-Waldenburg, handed us 10,000 marks. Our jubilation knew no bounds! Everyone gathered in the house, and we sang one song of praise and thanksgiving after another.

Now we had to tackle the practical problems. Necessary formalities such as the conveyance of title were already arranged, but there were plenty of other things that had to be planned. First we considered the upcoming potato harvest – our main food staple for the winter – and decided that the schoolchildren and teachers would bring it in. Next we formed a committee for remodeling and building construction led by Georg Barth. Adolf Braun (and later Arno Martin) was assigned to take on the farm work, including the plowing. The publishing house and the younger children were to remain in Sannerz for the time being, until accommodation was available. Adolf and Martha Braun were asked to be house parents for the new place, which we named the Rhön Bruderhof,[1] and Gertrud Ziebarth (later Dyroff) was sent to help them. Gertrud had joined us some time before; she served the community faithfully until her unexpected death in 1939, after the birth of her third son.

The first group of adults (and children from the age of twelve and up) moved to the new Bruderhof in time for the potato harvest. It was already November, with sharp north winds, rain, and fog, and they had to work speedily to beat the first hard frost. Martha, Moni, or I would go out with the children and bring along hot drinks for those who worked in the fields all day. Whenever the children's hands and feet grew too cold, we interrupted the work to dance in a circle. At night we put straw down in one of the rooms and slept on that. We also installed a small iron stove, though we had to stick the stove-pipe through a window, as there was no proper chimney. At least it was drier, if not much warmer, indoors.

While we dug potatoes in one field, the next was plowed in preparation for spring. Our farm equipment was in poor condition and needed continual repairs. Luckily we had a blacksmith, Fritz Kleiner, whose enthusiasm made him just the right man for this.

Aside from Georg, our construction team consisted mainly of young friends from the youth movement and the working class. Building was by no means easy without sufficient money or

---

[1] Bruderhof (German, "place of brothers") – the term used by the Hutterians of sixteenth-century Europe for their communal settlements.

materials. First we had to cut down trees; then we had to exchange the felled timber, which was obviously still green and unusable, for seasoned lumber in Veitsteinbach, the nearest village. Clay for the air-dried bricks, which we made ourselves, had to be hauled from Mittelkalbach, over an hour's trip downhill and an even longer one back uphill. Carting was done with two old horses that had come with our acquisition of the farmstead. During the day we used these horses for plowing, or for moving furniture and equipment up from Sannerz; at night we kept them busy, too, hauling up loads of material for the building. It was no surprise that one of them soon died, and that the other got sick and simply refused to carry on.

The horses we bought later, a lighter, East-Prussian breed, were also overworked. Hitched to a light buggy, which we had temporarily equipped for exhibiting books and pamphlets, they were used for mission and for transporting people to and from neighboring villages. They were also used for trips to the railroad stations – Sterbfritz, about an hour and a half away, or Neuhof, a little farther. Sometimes we even used them to pull the light carriage all the way to Fulda, about twenty miles away, since more often than not we had no money for the train. If someone needed cash in town, he first had to sell books or pamphlets, or small craft pieces like wooden candleholders, nativity scenes, and bookmarks.

I still remember a trip Else and I took just before Christmas one year: Else was driving, and we took just enough money to buy ourselves a hot cup of coffee on the way. Alas, Freia, our horse, went on strike halfway to Fulda, lying down in the middle of the road and refusing to respond, either to encouraging words or to cracks of the whip. She simply would not get up. Only when we gave her our coffee did she graciously get up and pull us the remaining twelve miles to Fulda. Yes, some days could be strenuous – but a little humor went a long way in lightening difficult moments.

Food at both Sannerz and the Rhön Bruderhof was very poor, and it is not surprising that the young men who worked on the building were often completely worn out. Everything was in short supply, and the few provisions we purchased had to be divided between the two households. Meat was very scarce, and the rations of bread, lard, and

Poor farm equipment and stony soil made plowing an arduous task at the Rhön Bruderhof—especially for overworked horses and undernourished men.

sugar inadequate. Potatoes were our main staple, but a good number had suffered from frost because of the late harvest, which gave them a sweetish taste. We did have some tough beef from an old cow, and there was plenty of fermented sauerkraut to be had. But in general there was no fat in the diet. Everyone could have eaten more, and the men who were working at the new farmstead in cold weather were especially hungry. A few times they even killed a cat (a "roof rabbit," the peasants joked) because they were so starved.

Eberhard and I spent two or three days a week on the farm. We would drive up on a sleigh, which was pleasant enough, but at times the fog and snow were so bad, we could not find the way. Several times we drove around in circles until one of the builders or men working in the fields heard our shouting. Once the snow was so deep we lost the road completely. To make things worse, it got dark early, and then we could not see anything at all.

Our presence was needed in many ways—giving encouragement, having personal talks, straightening out quarrels, or helping out where there was a lack of communication between various work crews. Often these troubles were related to our financial hardships,

Dancing around the May pole at the Rhön Bruderhof, 1927. Poverty was taken for granted, but it never got in the way of celebrations.

and then it seemed best to overcome them simply by singing them away. We sang humorous songs and songs of hope, as well as the old socialist songs like the one with the verse: "We're bound by love, we're bound by need / To fight for freedom and for bread."

Despite our poverty, some of our younger coworkers had a tremendous amount of idealism. Still, that was not always enough to overcome all the hardships. Thus several left us. Looking back, I do not think it was only because of the outward difficulties, though. Building up a new life made severe inner demands on us all; and as Jesus himself said, "Whoever of you does not renounce *all* that he has cannot be my disciple."

During this strenuous time our little school continued to function as well as it could, and the teachers even found time to put on a Christmas play with the children. The publishing work also went on, of course, as did our efforts at outreach. During the last week of December we hosted a conference of the Free German Youth at Sannerz, and one day we all walked to the new Bruderhof to hold a meeting there.

All in all, it was not easy to be separated into two groups: misunderstandings arose, and they had to be resolved by meeting to talk things over. A life in common, a life of sharing and working together! Even after all these years, I feel it is simply a mystery.

In the summer of 1927 it was finally possible for those of us who remained in Sannerz to move to the Rhön Bruderhof. It was a happy exodus, first for the fifteen remaining children, and some weeks later for the publishing staff. How joyful we were to be able to gather in *one* place again! We were still short of rooms, and some had to live in temporary quarters in a nearby barn. But what did that matter? It was summer, and we enjoyed living in nature.

That autumn we celebrated the engagement of Georg Barth and Monika von Hollander, the first in our community, and an occasion for lots of good fun, especially by the youth. On the morning after the engagement was announced, all the doors and windows were decorated with red hearts, and the old love song, "Who comes up the meadow way?" was sung, with new lines spontaneously added.

The wedding was celebrated on December 4, 1927. In spite of our great poverty – noodle soup was the main dish – it was a very joyful celebration. Red Christmas candles burned on a seven-armed candlestick that Georg himself had made, and the wedding ceremony and following celebration with coffee and stollen were very festive. Guests had been invited and came, among them Georg's sister Hilde.

Instead of taking traditional church vows, the couple answered questions taken from Zinzendorf, whose words on the meaning of love made a deep impression on all who were there:

"What special mystery does the church of God have?"

"Marriage."

"What does the mystery of marriage symbolize?"

"It is a symbol of Christ and the church."

Holding a burning red candle, Emy-Margret then recited a hymn by Methodius the Martyr, "From above, O virgins," with its chorus, "I dedicate myself to Thee, / And carrying a shining lamp / I go to meet Thee, Bridegroom." Rose Meyer recited Zinzendorf's poem, "We love each other truly," which includes a verse I have always especially liked:

O church, give thy ardent love completely,
With consecrated powers;
For God chose thee from eternity for love.
It is fitting that thy heart embrace
Both those who love thee and who hate thee.

Moni was several years older than Georg, but standing there in her white corduroy dress, a myrtle wreath in her hair, she looked younger than ever.

After all the festivities, the couple left for a short honeymoon in Würzburg – that beautiful old city, so rich in history and in architectural treasures inspired by reverence for Mary. The Barth's trip was made possible only with sacrifices; as usual, our finances were strained, and we were heavily in debt. Notes were due, and credit had to be extended, and Else, who had to get the papers in order for all this, made it just in time for the celebration.

I will always remember the Christmas season that followed – our first at the Rhön Bruderhof – as a very special one. In addition to the usual crib scene, we performed a play in which Georg took the part of Simeon, and I the part of Hannah. There were the old and new Christmas songs too, of course, and the hope that filled our hearts each year. How much we longed for the final Advent, the second coming of Christ when peace, joy, and justice will reign for all people!

The period between December 25 and January 1 was known among us in those days as the time "between the years," and we used it for meetings of clarification and renewal. Things that had disturbed the peace between individuals or in the community as a whole were straightened out, and other such matters settled and put to rest. It was also a time of reviewing the happenings of the past year and of looking forward into the future. In later years, when the farm and building work was very pressing, we would say to each other, "We'll have to talk this over some more under the Christmas tree."

That December, just "between the years" of 1927 and 1928, eleven-month-old Ursula Keiderling passed away. One minute the baby was playing happily in her bed; the next her mother Irmgard, who had left the room for a few minutes, returned to find the room full of smoke (a bundle of wet wood had been left drying near the stove) and the child breathing heavily. For the next twenty-four hours we stayed at the little girl's bedside, our hearts heavy with anxiety. The following evening, to our great shock and sorrow, she was taken from us.

After the little body was laid out in the publishing office, a small fir tree with burning candles was set by the bed; later we gathered around it and sang one Christmas lullaby after another: "Still, still, still, for Jesus goes to sleep" and "Let's rock the infant tender." A verse from the song, "Down over the mountain the wind's blowing mild" took on special meaning for us:

> The Baby awakens and looks up to heav'n.
> Then sing, all ye angels, rejoice, all ye men,
> For death now is vanquished, all pain and sin's might.
> Beloved and praised be God in the height!

On December 31 Eberhard and I went to Fulda, hoping to get permission to have the burial on our own land. Unfortunately we arrived at the licensor's office too late, and this plan did not work out. In the end we took the little body to the Catholic cemetery in Veitsteinbach, where we were allowed to hold our own service. Thus the year ended on a serious note, though the nearness of eternity brought us close together as well.

> In the midst of life are we
> By darkest death surrounded.
> Whom shall we seek to give us help?
> Where shall we find mercy?
> With thee alone, O God!

For a long time after 1922 we had fewer men among our ranks than women. Thus we were all the more joyful when, on the last day of 1927, two young co-workers, Hans Zumpe and Fritz Kleiner, publicly declared their intent to commit themselves for life to our common way. What an encouragement that was for the new year! Arno Martin had made the same decision a short while before, so we now had three young brothers who were able to shoulder greater responsibilities in the community.

1928 and 1929 brought new battles against the spirit of mammon and the powers of illness. With regard to our finances, it was the same old story as in Sannerz: notes became due, and we were not able to pay them, and two or three of us were constantly on the road in an effort to get our credit extended. This was very costly, both because of the time it took, and the high interest rates. Herr Schreiner, the local sheriff, came nearly every Friday to impound another piece of furniture (or a cow or pig) by affixing a "cuckoo" (a government-issue label with the German eagle on it) to it. Eberhard joked that the sheriff would not need to wait a year (as other guests who wanted to join us did) before becoming a member; after all, he was our guest every week! At one point the court even threatened to put the whole property up for sale by auction. Such drawbacks hampered our ability to build up as quickly as we would have liked to, but they never dampened our conviction. God had entrusted us with a task, and the work must go forward.

Ever since his university days, Eberhard had been fascinated with the radical Anabaptists of the Reformation period, and in the late 1920s this interest absorbed him and all of us once again. We were especially eager to learn all we could about the sixteenth-century Hutterites, for the origins of their communal settlements corresponded in so many ways to our own. Eberhard studied the history and economic basis of their communities, and at communal meals and meetings we read from their spiritual writings, and from accounts of their martyrs.

As further information about the early Hutterites was borrowed from libraries and archives, we realized how many aspects of their life were similar to ours: we read about their "orders" for communal living, their high standards of hygiene, and – for the sixteenth century, at least – their progressive educational practices. Not that we wanted to copy or imitate anything. Yet the more we found out, the closer we felt to them.

In essence, we already had the "services" of a traditional Hutterian community in our own. We had a servant of the Word (pastor), though not by that name; we had a brother to oversee business and financial matters, and another to oversee the work. We also had a housemother, a nurse, a sister who oversaw the practical work, a school principal, and several teachers. These tasks had not been designated as such—they had simply grown out of our life together. But it was the same spirit, calling us to the same witness in our time.

Some years earlier we had discovered that the Hutterites were still in existence in North America, but we had never initiated contact. Now, while talking in the publishing office one day, Fritz asked me, "What is it exactly that hinders us from working together with them?" In the discussions that followed, two things became clear: first, we strongly felt that all who sought to live in community of faith and work, in times past or present, must belong to the same ranks. Second, it was once again affirmed that Eberhard and Else and I had never wanted to "found" a movement of our own.

Before long, steps were taken toward a more concrete relationship with the Hutterites. We put together a document stating that we felt called to the same way of discipleship to which they had been called four hundred years earlier, and that we desired to be united with them. Eberhard sent the letter to a certain Elias Walter at a community in Alberta, and we eagerly awaited his reply. When after a long time an envelope arrived, we were somewhat sobered: it contained only a few booklets by Andreas Ehrenpreis, a seventeenth-century Anabaptist elder. Later, however, we did receive a short acknowledgment of our document. In 1929, letters began to flow more regularly, and as a result of the correspondence, Eberhard was invited to visit the Hutterian communities in Canada in 1930.

At the same time a dialogue was developing with the Hutterites, the energy that had awakened so many of our fellow German seekers to new life in the postwar years was subsiding. Yes, the Spirit was alive in some circles, such as the Neu-Sonnefeld and Eisenach Youth, and there were still similar groups in Switzerland, Holland, and England.

But there was much that had gone sour, too, especially in the *Siedlungen* or communal settlements that dotted the countryside. Many a commune disbanded as a result of disillusionment, erotic relationships, or fanaticism. Radical idealism was never lacking, but alas, most people were not ready to put their theories into practice.

Leadership was a critical problem in the youth movement: in some groups everyone wanted to determine his own lifestyle, his own work. Some believed that no one ought to be asked by another to do a certain job, and that freedom consisted in the right of each to do what he wanted, whenever he felt like it. People longed for community, yet it was not unusual to hear comments such as, "We have worked under the whip far too long" or "We did not join a settlement just to be ordered around by others" or even "We recognize no authority here." At our Bruderhof, too, the question of freedom and its true meaning was a frequent theme in meetings.

Guests continued to come, and we were grateful for every one who stayed. Katrin Ebner, a peasant woman from nearby, came to us with her baby, Anna, and was soon a fully committed member. She was the only one to join us from the immediate neighborhood. Gretel Knott (later Gneiting), a kindergarten teacher, joined us in 1928 – another wonderful addition to our community.

Numerous communists visited us in those years. Some of them were overwhelmed with what they found. Calling us *Edelkommunisten* ("noble communists"), they said our life embodied their philosophy's deepest ideals. Others left us full of indignation, especially over our rejection of violence. These told us, "When communism rules the land, you will be the first to hang." Eberhard expressed our belief that as followers of the way of Jesus, we could never resort to violence; nevertheless, we continued to share our conviction that communism and socialism had a vital message for the world, and especially for so-called Christians. Institutional religion was only a stumbling block, for among the established churches, there was not one that had not made common cause with wealth and worldly power. "And if the disciples are silent, the very stones will cry out."

Guests from nationalistic circles came to us, too; I remember long discussions with them about the question of national interest above self-interest, and about *Volksgemeinschaft* ("national community"), a concept the Nazis would make familiar in their own twisted way in years to come. Even though we searched for common ground with these guests, there were heated arguments.

The growing popularity of nationalistic ideas held by men like Hitler can be partly understood in the context of this time. Certainly, the war was long over, but Germans were still suffering from the economic ravages of defeat. Food was scarce and prices were high, imported goods were unaffordable, and high unemployment rates created unrest in the larger cities. (At this point I must pay tribute to the help the English Quakers gave so many schools and hospitals, orphanages, and old people's homes throughout those difficult years.) Inflation was not what it had been in the worst years, 1923 and 1924, but paper currency was still undervalued. No wonder that, with all these hardships, people sought a leader to restore order to the country, and that they cared little about his political leanings.

As time went on, more needy children were brought to us. One day the police asked us if we would take an abandoned two-year-old. They had found him hanging in a sack from a tree by the roadside, with a note: "Whoever finds this child may keep it." Adolf and Martha Braun (who had two children of their own) took the boy into their family.

Erhard, (as he turned out to be named), had been neglected—he was covered with lice and scabies, and underfed. Under Martha's care he soon thrived, however. As he grew older, we noticed a certain restlessness in him, an urge to rove and ramble, and sometimes he even ran away, though never for long. Unfortunately, some time after Hitler came to power a dark, swarthy man showed up on a bicycle one day, claiming he was the boy's father and producing an official paper to that effect. What could we do? The stranger took Erhard with him, and it was the last time we saw the boy.

Then there was "Ulala," another child the gypsies brought to us when he was still a baby. Moni raised Ulala and loved him dearly, but he too was taken back by his family when he was older. They lived in a trailer in a poor area near Fulda, which we visited in an effort to get the boy back, but in vain. Later we heard he died in a Catholic institution.

Walter was one-and-a-half when his mother brought him to us because of unhappy family circumstances. We took him into our own family, and Else faithfully looked after him. After a while he returned to his mother, but Else was eventually able to bring him back and legally adopt him.

In the meantime our own children were growing up, and we began to look into the possibility of further education for them outside the Bruderhof. For one thing, we wanted them to find a field or trade that could support them once they were adults. Even more important, we wanted each to be able to make an independent decision regarding their future. We wanted no lame, half-hearted companions on the narrow way we had chosen – neither in our own families, nor among the children we took in and brought up.

To begin with, Emy-Margret was to start training as a kindergarten teacher at a Froebel school at Thale in the Harz Mountains. Hardy went to Bieberstein, a boarding school that taught farming and crafts as well as academic subjects, and Hans Grimm was apprenticed to a carpenter for three years. There were others, too, of course, but only till 1933, when Nazi repression put an end to it all.

During the first years at the Rhön Bruderhof we were all involved in the agricultural work. We had a trained gardener – Walter Hüssy, a religious socialist who joined us from Switzerland in 1929 – but he could only do so much. The Sparhof had been neglected so long, and the soil was so poor to begin with, that farming never really provided a sufficient basis for a livelihood.

Garden vegetables ripened late because of the high altitude of the Rhön and the prevailing cold winds, and the potatoes came to an end in spring, after which our food was always especially meager until the next harvest came in. We grew our own wheat, but it was barely enough to last us the six months from fall to spring. On top of that we had no money to buy bread. I still remember how, after a guest donated fifty marks, we sent one of the children to the village to buy bread straight away! At birthdays, a loaf of bread replaced the cake – and many preferred it.

In a 1928 "letter to our guests," a sort of house rule given to each visitor, we advised anyone who insisted on having bread to provide his own, as our harvest was poor and we could not promise suffi-

The Rhön Bruderhof dining room decorated for Advent, 1930. Lighting was provided by the seven-armed candelabras hanging from the ceiling.

cient food—not even for our own members. Some found this hard to accept. Simplicity, they said, they could understand. But bread? That was a basic necessity, and surely it was not asking too much to have enough on hand. But at times that was simply the way things were.

In one of our favorite songs ("We plough the fields and scatter"), instead of the lines, "He gives the cattle pasture / And to our children bread," we sometimes sang, "He gives the children pasture / And to our cattle bread." It was no joke, really—while the cows were fed as much grain as possible to ensure good milk for the children, the rest of us had to be content with meal after meal of wild meadow spinach.

When (for the first time after many years) we had hogs to slaughter and were able to add pork to our diet, many of us got upset stomachs. We simply were not used to meat anymore.

The health of several was poor, and not only because of malnutrition. Else, who had lost half of her stomach through an operation, suffered from tuberculosis, as did Emy-Margret. During one especially bad period, the doctors gave Else only a few days to live, yet when we prayed for her, she recovered, and before we knew it she was back at work, resuming a full schedule as Eberhard's secretary.

To improve our long-term food situation we decided to plant windbreaks on the hill behind our houses, where only heather was growing. In the fall of 1932, with the aid of a Baptist youth group who came to staff a "work camp," we set out hundreds of spruce and larch saplings. We also planted cherry, plum, and apple trees.

In spite of the hardships of these years, our children's community had kept growing, and in 1928 we had built a new children's house. Thanks to a friendly local official, District Administrator von Gagern, we were able to secure a favorable long-term building loan from the government. Georg drew up the plans and Fritz supervised the actual operation. There was tremendous excitement the day we finally broke ground (on the site of a dilapidated old barn), and the whole community gathered to celebrate. What a joy it was to see the walls of this first self-built house go up on our land, regardless of the shortage of cash!

For the opening of the children's house we invited officials from Kassel and Fulda. It happened to be the day the court had previously set for an auction of our property, but luckily this was averted at the last minute by an unexpected gift of 5,000 Swiss francs from a friend. I still remember the song we sang at this dedication cere-

(L to R) Emmy, Luise Kolb, Monika Arnold, Else von Hollander, and her adopted son Walter relax near the newly built Children's House, Rhön Bruderhof, 1930.

mony – the old German student ballad, "We built up a house that was stately and strong," with its courageous vision for the future, no matter the odds:

The house may be ruined –
We count not the loss;
The Spirit lives among us
And our stronghold is God.

Some four years earlier, Eberhard had shared with our circle a dream of his own: he visualized a day when all manner of people – industrialists, professionals, workers, teachers, washerwomen, and the poorest of the poor – would come to us in a great procession, all wanting to live in community. Eberhard not only hoped for such a day; he firmly believed it would come. Therefore our main task, he said, was to make room for all these people, to build up a future home for them.

At first I could not grasp this at all. Yes, we were planning to eventually buy all seven farmsteads of the Sparhof, and to gradually improve them. But even after this was achieved, I did not see how we could possibly accommodate and support more than 200 to 250 people. Eberhard, on the other hand, had no patience for such worries: his vision for the future sprang from faith, not from human calculations and projections.

Sometimes I felt like the hunter in a popular folk song, who sings: "I cannot keep up with your long, high leaps." I said this in a meeting, too, so everyone could know how I felt, and at the next mealtime, this refrain was sung over and over to tease me: "Hu-sa-sa, trala-la-la / I cannot keep up with your long, high leaps!" Some time later, during a visit to my husband's mother in Breslau, we were able to talk things over thoroughly, and Eberhard and I came to a complete understanding. I shall never forget those lively talks as we walked in the park.

In those years of building up we often read in our meetings about the moving of the spirit in past centuries. The more we steeped ourselves in the Radical Reformation of the sixteenth-century, the more it appealed to all of us. Here we sensed a communal spirit that pervaded every aspect of life and carried over right into the struggle for peace, justice, and equality. The writings of Hans Denck, Balthasar Hubmaier, and other Anabaptists especially captivated us, but also those of Thomas Münzer, an outstanding fighter for the suffering people of his day. To us, Münzer was no different from leaders of the working class movement in our own time, men such as Hermann Kutter, Leonhard Ragaz, and (until his death in 1919) Gustav Landauer.

Like the early Anabaptists—and like these contemporary radicals—we did not feel that protesting was enough, though we did that, too. (After Walter Rathenau and Kurt Eisner were assassinated, for instance, we participated in marches and rallies against political murder.[2]) We were determined to find positive answers to the crises of our time, and again and again we found them in the building up of a life of brotherhood for all men and women.

---

[2] Kurt Eisner (b. 1867), socialist president of Bavaria murdered in 1919; Walter Rathenau (b. 1867), German Secretary of State murdered by right-wing radicals, 1922.

American Journey

The time for a journey to North America came closer. Eberhard was corresponding with the Hutterites in South Dakota and Manitoba, and our small circle was eager to send him, and perhaps a second person, to visit them for six months. From the first, we felt a reverence for their four centuries of communal living; and as I have already said, the many things we read about their history gave us a sense of belonging to them.

After the crisis of 1922 we had often felt isolated, even though people continued to join us, and we cherished the hope that through our contact with the Hutterian movement, new horizons would open for us. Then, too, there were our continuing financial straits, and our hope that the American Hutterites would be willing to share with fellow believers. Though some of the letters that came from them encouraged us in this regard, others were disappointing, so we did not know what to expect from this trip. Were today's Hutterites still guided by the same spirit of radical faith-based communism as their forebears?

It was characteristic of our life in those years that nothing was won without struggle, and so it was with this trip to America. Early in 1930, Eberhard had a severe inflammation in his left eye, which was practically blind. He had injured it many years before in a skiing accident, and again later in Sannerz, when a splinter flew into it while he was chopping wood and caused detachment of the retina.

In May, just before Eberhard's departure from Germany, the eye became inflamed again. Despite this he continued to prepare for his journey, especially by studying further his growing collection of old Hutterian writings. The eye grew worse, and I insisted on taking Eberhard to the doctor. While there, I was called into the office and advised to keep my husband from taking such a long journey with his eye in as poor condition as it was. Eberhard would not hear of it.

Farewell at the Fulda station, May 1930. Eberhard's eye is heavily bandaged, and Emmy has been crying. With no telephone, North America seemed worlds away from Europe.

"Do let me go!" he pleaded. "We've always dared everything in faith!"

The day before he left, Eberhard baptized nine new members at a spring in our woods. The next morning Else and I accompanied him as far as Fulda, where we met our son, Hardy, who had traveled down from Bieberstein to see his father off. And so he set out.

Naturally we were all eager to hear what Eberhard would find in the Hutterian communities. Unfortunately, though we received dozens of letters from him, they were a long time coming. Transatlantic mail went only by ship in those days and usually took many weeks. Cables were expensive, and very rare. Often we felt completely out of touch.

I will not write about the Hutterites and our contact with them in detail here, since Eberhard's own words tell best what all he experienced.[1] The excerpts that follow are from his letters to me:

On board the S.S. Karlsruhe, June 1 and 2, 1930.

My eye is supposed to heal by the time I reach New York. I am diligently treating it and have faith in Christ, who wants to make the inner light good to be a light for the body, and the outer eye for the way. The kingdom must always be first for us.

Chicago, June 18, 1930.

At last my eye is so much better that today I have had practically no pain at all. In New York and Scottdale, Pennsylvania, the love of the very faithful and very punctual and very earnest

---

[1] For a full account of Eberhard's year among the Hutterites in Canada, and the story of their relationship with the Bruderhof as documented with Eberhard's diaries and letters, see the book *Brothers Unite* (Farmington, PA: Plough, 1988).

Mennonites left me no time, and even less strength, for writing. So I squeezed in one day in an expensive hotel. I am spending the day in my room, with no intention of going out at all, in order to think and write in quiet to you, to the children, and to the whole faithful Bruderhof, and also to take care of my eye.

The services of the Mennonite Church last many hours and are amazingly lively. The Bible is read in enormously long sections. The last hour–exactly sixty minutes–was given to me. As a message for the Mennonites, I took our special theme: the event of Pentecost in Jerusalem with all its consequences. I strongly emphasized Christ's gospel and then spoke about complete love and community, in which everything belongs to God and to the community of the Spirit. On their express wish I then told about my personal development, about you and Halle, Leipzig, and Berlin. I witnessed to the Sermon on the Mount and tried to awaken their religious-social conscience...

At the end I told about Sannerz and the Rhön Bruderhof, and about the children's community, emphasizing that it was not my task to bear witness to our Bruderhof, but that our Bruderhof has to bear witness to the outpouring of the Holy Spirit, with all its consequences. I closed by reciting Emy-Margret's song. At the final words, "And Jesus Christ before them goes, / And after him run all who can," I *ran* back to my seat, and joyful laughter closed the talk.

According to John Horsch [a Mennonite historian and friend of the Hutterites who helped arrange Eberhard's travel plans] it should not be hard for me to understand the language of the Hutterites. Their Tyrolean-Bavarian dialect will not be a problem, but my all-too-abstract German may be difficult for them. Well, perhaps I will come home a simple peasant, also in speech.

He has also told me many good things about the leaders of the Hutterites...It is true that one of them, David Hofer of Rockport, has been cautious and cool regarding my upcoming visit to the communities, but that may be on account of my fundraising hopes. David apparently estimates that to finance a Bruderhof takes $250,000, which is more than a million marks. Well, I can see why he would be worried about that! Let's hope I will be able to find the right way. But the main thing is our witness to unity in the Spirit!

Harold Bender wrote a good letter to the Hutterites on our behalf, sharing his impressions of us. He calls us true Baptizers in the Hutterian sense, and describes our poverty and our communal life; he writes about our rejection of modern liberalism and about our Biblicism, which, he agrees, is far removed from pietism and is rather a matter of honest conviction. He said that with us there is deed as well as words, which moves him very deeply.

Tabor, South Dakota, June 24, 1930.

The brothers and sisters are very kind to me and send love to you all. The spirit and reality of today's Hutterianism far surpasses my expectations. There is a living relationship with God, and a deep faith in the Holy Spirit and in Christ's redemption. They are well aware of the church's need for the Holy Spirit to come to us and speak to us again and again. Good discipline is kept by speaking openly, not behind a person's back. Joy and cheerfulness are constantly expressed in good-natured joking, and on a deeper level in quoting words of faith from the Bible, from popular proverbs or past experiences. The simplicity of the life is still fairly pure. For example, no Bruderhof has a car, nor does anyone wish to buy one. The older people, but also many of the younger ones, have deep joy in their life and in the flaring fire of first love that leads to community. Still, their material wealth is hard for me to understand.

Wolf Creek, South Dakota, July 15, 1930.

The doctor has been treating my eye for weeks, but has not yet allowed reading or writing...But I believe the days are not lost. From my bed I experienced the daily life of the people here in a special way, and could take it in and reflect on everything that came my way. The faith of the Hutterites is real and genuine. It is deeply rooted in the hearts of all. They do not want to – they cannot – live any other way than in community. The practical forgetting of self in the service of the community is far stronger than with us. The seriousness of the divine witness to the truth is strong even in the simplest members. Their prayer life is touching. It moved me particularly when I was Michel Waldner's guest and slept in his room: I saw the old man praying in the dark by his big wooden chest, his knees bent, his hands held up to God before his face with a wonderful dignity and reverence. It is the early Christian attitude of prayer...

America has not lived through the judgment of a world war or revolution, and the social conscience of the people is not awake. There is no feeling for God's kingdom and his justice, and one preaches to deaf ears. Mammon reigns undisputed over the religious and the irreligious alike. All the same the Hutterites are conscious of their lack of missionary outreach. Perhaps because of this they expect more from us than we have to give...David [Hofer] said recently, "If Arnold has come from Germany to look for what we had in the old days, he will be very dissatisfied with us, if only because of our great possessions in land and money." He is very much distressed about the way things have developed...

Rockport, South Dakota, July 26, 1930.

The task I have here is too great to be accomplished in a short time. You know that I am not by nature slow to fulfill a duty once recognized, especially in the face of pressing need. But my quickness to act has not always been a good thing!

Lake Byron, South Dakota, August 5, 1930.

The confirmation of my leadership as an Hutterian servant of the Word [pastor] is coming closer. When I think of the twelve articles of the Apostolic creed and of Peter Rideman's momentous *Confession*...I feel my own weakness and sinfulness so strongly that I would like to see someone else from our circle in this position. But I dare not shirk it.

Winnipeg, Manitoba, August 1930.

Peter Hofer [a Hutterite minister] says repeatedly that the awakening, vitalizing, and unifying of American Hutterianism will have to come through us. And Joseph, the younger Kleinsasser [another minister] emphasizes—probably too much—that my visit and our "new zeal" has great significance for them. Joseph Kleinsasser, the group's elder, acknowledges that our beginning is right, especially in those areas where he feels we are more radical, and more Hutterian, than his own people. But he is against forcing the establishment of formal ties...He is a man of faith, of the Spirit, a man who really seems to depend entirely on God.

Winnipeg, August 25, 1930.

The promises of financial help that I have been able to confirm… are still few and far between. David Hofer of James Valley and Joseph Waldner of Huron, two of the most important representatives of the movement here, feel we have been tested and proven sufficiently by the fact that we have lasted several years and preserved our orders. They are enthusiastic about our basis and feel that for my confirmation I need only answer the questions prescribed by their order.

Most nights I have open discussions with members of the various communities here until midnight, sometimes until one o'clock. That is where I receive the strongest impressions of the faith, love, and firmness of the brothers and sisters. They all take part in these discussions and are eager to hear anything I can tell them about you.

Winnipeg, September 4, 1930.

I can't describe to you the deep joy I feel when I read your wonderful letters. I wish I could answer them all…In contrast to Germany, the elderly people here are for the most part much more lively. But many of the young adults begin their long search to attain the same depth of faith only at baptism…There are definite problems among the youth, and I do not think fears of a threatening decline are unfounded.

The love and gratitude with which I am welcomed here is proof of a longing, of faith, and of pulsating life. I am embarrassed when people say I should become the leader for all communities, so as to draw them together and lead them in mission. I know only too well that I would be the wrong person for this…

They all say, "You pray for mission, but your Bruderhof with its guests is mission." Their understanding of mission is to seek out the "zealous"—and only these—to challenge and gather them, and call them home. David Hofer of Rockport said, "If the church is right, then there will be mission, if not, there will be none." People here feel we should stay in Germany as long as we can maintain our zeal, and as long as school authorities and other government agencies do not hamper our efforts…

To summarize, let me say that even today's Hutterites, with all their weaknesses, are so unique in their almost perfect communal life, their simplicity and modesty, that as far as we know there is nothing in Europe that even approaches it. Everything we expected from the Fellowship Movement, the youth movement, and the Religious Socialists can be found here, though again, as with every group, there are unmistakable signs of weakness.

Cardston, Alberta, October 2, 1930.

Today is the 2nd of October, that day in 1899 when I had the first conscious encounter with our Savior and Redeemer Jesus Christ. At that time you too, as a child, were already deeply impressed by our beloved Jesus, and gave yourself to him completely. I am confident that the uniting with the Hutterites will bring to you and me and all of us the fulfillment of faith's longing of so many years.

Lethbridge, Alberta, October 8, 1930.

Now I am going through what you predicted: that I would not be able to bear for long the separation from you, from our children, from our home, and from our dear, faithful brothers and sisters... But I must and will hold out.

Here in Lethbridge, as elsewhere, the Hutterites are very loving and interested, and have very warm hearts for our cause. And yet still, up to this day, I can hardly speak about the pressing need of our financial situation, a need that is unknown here. Everybody is of the opinion, with the well-known rigid firmness of the Hutterites, that the things of the spirit must come first, and only then the temporal can be considered. Where I can do so without hurting our cause, I bring up the issue of the $25,000 I would like to bring home at Christmas. Hutterian naiveté responds with earnest eyes: "So much all at once?"

Lethbridge, October 23, 1930.

You will be worried by now [that I have not written for so long], and indeed it was my eye again. The treatment cost a whole week and $35...

I want to visit the communities again, more slowly this time. If I go too fast, it immediately puts the strain on my eye—especially if I have to share a bed with old Andreas [an elderly minister]! At the same time I am pursued and overwhelmed by all the love. I am worried that they expect too much of me. On the other hand, they are giving me a wealth of old writings to bring home, which will be a great help to us in our publishing work.

Milford, Alberta, October-November 1930.

Today I am to travel to a community near Wilson – in a closed car, as riding in an open wagon with a brisk wind has done my eye no good. You can imagine that the enthusiasm of all the brothers and sisters who come thronging to me at every place doesn't give me a minute of rest. This is not a complaint. As Johannes Wurz says, we should thank God that such an awakening has come about through my visit, from which many (though not all) expect a spiritual renewal…The worst part of it is that my departure date has come into question because of urgent requests from Elias Walter. Please don't do anything to hinder this. Every fiber in me is urging me homewards, but the goal of this costly and strenuous journey must not be endangered by our impatience and longing.

Crow's Nest, British Columbia, November 30, 1930.

Emmy in an Hutterian dress sent to her by Eberhard from Canada, October 1930.

I can hardly endure it anymore to be separated from you for so long, and to be so far away from the beloved circle of our old and new, faithful co-fighters – from the unique spirit and life of our Bruderhof. At practically all communities the meetings have been wonderful, with hours of uninterrupted attentiveness and enthusiasm. I am so much sought after that neither in Lethbridge nor in Macleod, Cardston, nor Calgary, nor even in smaller places, have I had so much as half a day's rest for writing, without being found out and taken somewhere. The brothers and sisters are easily hurt if a "guest from so far away, and one who lives in real community," has no time for a brotherly talk!

The Rockies, Nov. 26, 1930.

How happy, how joyful I am for the clear guidance you have been given through the Holy Spirit during all these months. How faithfully you have responded to the brothers and sisters of the communities, once led by Jakob Hutter with the glowing fire of love and with equally fiery discipline! In the same way you have courageously accepted their well-tested traditions and orders, with minimal questioning, which humanly speaking would have been quite understandable. And now you have a veritable treasury of writings that radiate the Spirit–dozens and dozens of hand-written books, pamphlets, and leaflets, among them more than fifty very old pieces. Few if any of the communities here have such a precious collection of old handwritings.

The brothers' love to us is so great that they surely will not let us down as regards our requests for financial help. However, with their persistent thoroughness, all this will take time...Be assured that I will come home as quickly as possible–as soon as my task of finding unity and support for my service and for the economy of our Bruderhof is completed, at least to a certain degree.

Trust that you will all be guided through everything in unity through God's Spirit. Be openhearted and ready for one another. Have joy in one another! You have every reason for this. Together with your youthfulness in God, preserve your feeling for purity and unity in the Spirit. But become free, and remain free, from touchiness, from worrying that you may be treated differently from others, also in your duties and services! There is really no cause for this.

Rejoice that you are all different, and do not try to make every-one's special qualities equal and uniform–that would only para-lyze and extinguish them. Community is alive only when there is living reciprocity. Therefore rejoice in your diversity and never resent it...Yes, there are things that can never be allowed: selfish-ness and pettiness, gossiping, envy and jealousy, fear and worry. Like self-seeking and self-will, these cause nothing but loss and damage. But no one has so few gifts as to make himself totally useless through his concern with these trivialities. I plead with you, persevere and stand together in unity and love and joy. Don't waste a single meeting on discussions that would be unnecessary if you stood together more faithfully, more firmly, more trust-ingly, and more gratefully...

I earnestly ask you: Carry your great and holy responsibility steadfastly, like a burning light in your hands. For the sake of this light, do not let yourselves be pushed, shaken, or knocked over! Then the radiance of your burning candles will shine over to me as in a vision, and will strengthen me and lead me back with everything you need. You know that the incarnation of the Creator and his word of love, and Jesus' words and work through the outpouring of his Spirit, is the strength in which you can do everything.

Therefore let no foreign, dark, unclear, or apathetic spirit enter among you, not even through guests, relatives, old and new friends, or other visitors. Let nothing, not the slightest thing, come among you that offends Jesus Christ, his redemption of the world, his humility in the manger and on the cross, his outpoured Spirit of unity and purity.

Lethbridge, for Christmas and for your birthday.

Our sacrifices are finally bearing fruit. God, who guides everything, has used even my infected eye to move the brothers so that at last they are opening their cautious hearts to the cause entrusted to us in Germany…And so I write to you as a real Hutterian brother.

On December 9, the brothers unanimously decided to accept me and incorporate me into the Hutterian Church. I will write about this in detail as soon my confirmation as a servant of the Word has taken place [December 17]…

The fact that I have been taken in as a member should mean that we will be taken care of as brothers and sisters, that the time of begging for alms should be over, and that the time for building up and for mission should begin.

Because of the injection for my eye treatment, I cannot write more today. May God grant that I may return to you soon, and with answers to the many needs of our Bruderhof…

So far, the following has been arranged and planned: Each debt-free community is to contribute $1000 to our cause; and each half-indebted community $500. Completely indebted communities will not be expected to contribute. In addition to this, thirty high-grade work horses are to be sent overseas, and fifteen high-grade milk cows.

Stand Off, Alberta, December 25 and 31, 1930.

There is no other course for me than to travel once more through the Alberta communities to gather the sums we need. It will be very strenuous for me...my nervous system and my body, and perhaps also my inner life have not adjusted to all this traveling. I am totally exhausted. Yet I must gather all my strength to carry on with raising the funds necessary for our building up.

Old Christian, the minister who presided at the big confirmation meeting of twenty-one servants, is unwilling to give more significant support, as his Bruderhof has exhausted its funds in a large purchase of land. There is only one way of storming these fortresses, and that is to besiege them continuously, like the persistent widow...

Lethbridge, February 1931.

I have visited twelve more communities, though only with partial success. Our beloved Bruderhof! For me it is still the best, the only possible one. I have been deeply convinced of that here, also that we should remain in Germany as long as possible, in part because the people of Europe are again struggling and suffering so much.

Lethbridge, February 1931.

The fund-raising is moving forward again, though slowly—so slowly that I would give up hope of ever gathering what we need, were it not for the higher faith that guides me. So I must persist.

Lethbridge, March 1931.

Now my departure is finally here! There is my worn-out Hutterian suit and two hats for our "museum." Also to be saved for the museum—and not used—is a broom made and presented to me by Jakob of Old Elm Spring, who is over seventy.

South Dakota, April 10, 1931.

One thing I know: I will never again undertake such a journey alone, without you! True, I have found the best of care wherever I went. But it was very hard to be so far away from that singularly fresh spirit of Sannerz and the Rhön Bruderhof.

Radio-telegram, May 1, 1931.

On the ship at last! Meet me Bremerhaven Sunday, May 10. Happy, your Eberhard.

Eberhard surrounded by onlookers at a Bruderhof in Alberta, Canada, 1931.

Eberhard's reception by the Hutterites varied considerably from place to place. He deeply appreciated the love and trust shown him by most of the communities; yet on the other hand, he was troubled by many things he saw. For one, there seemed to be little real sharing beyond that within a given community. Some farms were large and well-to-do, while others were poor and deeply in debt. The question of technology was also a difficult one for him; he felt it that in some quarters at least, it was the machine that controlled the man, and not man the machine. Worse, the Hutterite communities were divided into three separate groups or *Leut* ("people"). How, he asked, could this possibly be in keeping with the Spirit, with the love that gives and shares everything, the love from which a unified church community can arise and endure?

Eberhard spoke many times to the Hutterites about all these things, especially on the basis of their own early writings. After all, aside from their embrace of more modern farming methods, they were very tradition-bound, especially in outward forms such as their peasant-style costumes. In reaction to the Catholic liturgy, they rejected not only the organ and piano, but even flutes, fiddles and guitars. As for photographs, they quoted the Old Testament prohibition against graven images (yet forgot its main point: "You shall not worship them!") Eberhard had many discussions about these things, for they seemed unnecessarily harsh, but the elders would not yield.

Of course, they also questioned him about our practices, in particular smoking. Remarkably, they did not object to alcohol, something we could have understood; though as the case was, we were too poor to have any. Naturally, when these and many other questions came to our attention through Eberhard's letters, it gave us pause. Much as we felt we had to learn from the Hutterites, we did not want to place ourselves under laws and regulations that were not born out of our own living experience.

Interestingly, though we appreciated all of the old, handwritten manuscripts Eberhard was given, we found the writings of their earliest sixteenth-century founders most striking; they, on the contrary, preferred the less pithy, more pietistic teachings of later forebears, and felt these were better suited to their life.

When our incorporation into the Hutterian Church was confirmed in December 1930, we tried with Eberhard to do justice to their sixteenth-century origins. We were keenly aware of the streams that had influenced our own beginnings: the revival movement, the Free German Youth, religious-socialism, and the ferment in the working class. But we also saw that, as products of our own confused times, these movements had their defects and lacked eternal meaning in many ways.

Not everything that went with the uniting was easy for us. The Hutterite costume for women, with its head covering or *Kopftuch*, was not hard for us to accept. Indeed, we were glad to adopt the simple peasant style. The brothers' dress was a different matter. We did not like the required blacks and dark grays, but preferred the brighter colors of the youth movement. All the same, it was not a question of conscience, and we were willing to take on anything that might further our unity.

Giving up photographs and musical instruments seemed to us a much greater sacrifice. Pictures could often say much more than words! And hiking together with flutes and guitars...and all the beautiful folk songs and songs of religious awakening—all this belonged to our life. Still, how could we refuse to yield on this or that point—to re-think everything—if it led to greater unity with others? Wasn't that of far greater worth? We mulled over such questions often during Eberhard's absence.

In general, things at home went smoothly enough during Eberhard's year away, though we missed him dearly and often ached to be with him. Hans Zumpe, then twenty-three, had been asked to take Eberhard's place, and the rest of us tried to support him as best we could. Certainly life was not without struggles. Ambition and arrogance – the perpetual enemies of community life – raised their heads soon after Eberhard had left, and several times we had to occupy ourselves with our weaknesses. But Hans saw the way clearly and kept to it with love and firmness. As always, we were confident that if a problem was taken up unitedly – that is, in the spirit that seeks a common solution – it could be overcome.

Many guests came in the summer of 1930; in particular I remember a work camp we hosted for Erich Mohr and his Free German Youth. With the help of our brothers, the work campers drained a wet meadow, and we had had many lively discussions with them. All in all, however, it did not lead to much. For many of them, vegetarianism seemed to be the consuming issue.

Eberhard's letters were received with great interest, and we read each of them in our meetings. From time to time money came too, as often as he was able to send it, and this was a great help in stopping some of the gaps. But as usual we were still extremely short of money.

On our wedding anniversary, December 20, news came via cable that the uniting with all three Hutterite groups – the *Lehrerleut, Dariusleut,* and *Schmiedeleut*–had taken place. There was great rejoicing, also because Eberhard's return now seemed imminent. But the next news tempered our happiness: he planned to visit all the communities again to beg for funds.

When Eberhard finally did return the next spring, we were disappointed at the overall results of his strenuous efforts. In the end, considering their circumstances, the forty-odd Hutterite communities had given precious little toward our building up. But we had no choice, no desire, except to continue, even if the work was laborious and slow. For us, every new day we could share was pure joy.

9

Between Time
and Eternity

Eberhard's long awaited return on May 10, 1931, was a tremendous joy and strengthening. Hans Zumpe and I went to Bremerhaven to meet him on May 9, for the ship was expected as early as six o'clock the next morning. We stood on the dock and watched the ship approaching from a distance. There were many people on the decks, waving to their relatives, but hard as we tried we could not see Eberhard. Finally we discovered him, standing alone in the stern of the ship. In all the joy of being safely home, the fact that he had returned without the hoped for financial help for the community was still a burden to him. Yet what a reunion after a whole year's absence! There was so much we had to tell each other, first with Hans, and then the two of us alone.

Else, unfortunately, was not there. She was suffering from tuberculosis again, and (through the kindness of our friend Friedrich Wilhelm Foerster) convalescing in the home of a friend in Switzerland. Else stayed on in this home until July, for we knew that as soon as she returned, her work as Eberhard's secretary would completely consume her.

Emy-Margret and Hardy were both home when their father arrived; she had passed her exams as kindergarten teacher the previous fall, and he had finished his last year at the *Gymnasium* (secondary school) at Easter. Having been away for three years, Hardy was to help in the farm work for a year before going on to Tübingen University. Both children had decided to stay with the community and had become members, which was a great encouragement to Eberhard and me.

In one of the first members' meetings after Eberhard's return, we decided on wedding dates for the four engaged couples in our

Else von Hollander in Tirol, 1913, when she began to care for the Arnold children and assist Eberhard as his secretary—tasks she devoted herself to for the rest of her life.

circle: Leo Dreher and Trautel Fischli, Alfred Gneiting and Gretel Knott, Hans Zumpe and Emy-Margret Arnold, and Walter Hüssy and Trudi Dalgas.

Preparing a living space for each one was easier said than done, since we constantly had to find accommodations for new members and children as well, and there were very few resources available. Much of the money sent home by Eberhard over the course of his year away had been used to pay outstanding debts; on top of this, several creditors had been put off until his return.

Nevertheless, we were able to set up a room for each of the new couples. We made the furniture ourselves, all in the same plain style, but stained different shades of red, rust, and brown. The rooms were painted in bold colors—orange, yellow, light green. Each couple had a bed, a table, a corner bench, two chairs, and a washstand. Bright curtains hung at the windows.

Hans and Emy-Margret's wedding took place in July and was crowned by the joy of having Else home again from Switzerland. She was no longer able to work full-time, but she did what she could, typing up letters and minutes of meetings. Sometimes she did this in a deck chair outdoors; later she grew so weak that she could only work from her bed, in a little hut that had been fixed up especially for her.

Although the help expected from our new North American brothers had not materialized, 1931–1932 was the period of greatest growth since our communal life had begun. The building went ahead feverishly, sometimes on three sites at once. Two new houses were built, as well as a pigsty, a horse stable, and a bakery. New workshops were set up too. All the money that came in was used for construction; nothing was left in the bank. Each day brought new joys. After so many years when much time and energy had gone into simply obtaining enough money to keep afloat, we were finally building up!

New families joined us from Switzerland, first Hans and Else Boller and then Peter and Anni Mathis in 1932 and Hans and Margrit Meier in early 1933. The latter two families came from the Werkhof, a religious-socialist community near Zurich. Single young people from Switzerland came too: Lini Rudolf, Margot Savoldelli, and Julia Lerchy. All of these new members were a great help in our building up; unbelievably, they also brought with them a combined sum of money that matched almost exactly the amount we had hoped to receive from the Hutterites.

Others came too – short- and long-term guests, and people who wanted to join us for good, among them Annemarie Wächter (who later married our son Heinrich) and Ria Kiefer. Nils Wingaard and Dora Sääf, both Swedes, came to us as an engaged couple shortly after Eberhard's return and decided to stay; they were married in the autumn of 1932. Friedel Sondheimer, one of our first Jewish members, came during Eberhard's absence.

Many guests came with difficult personal needs or unusual worldviews. People with illnesses, including some with mental illness, came seeking help. Individual cases are difficult to report; it is perhaps enough to say that there were both victories and defeats.

How stimulating and exciting they were, those evenings we spent with them under the great beech tree on the brow of the hill behind our house! Sometimes the discussions centered on issues brought up by our visitors and new members: national socialism, for example, and vegetarianism; education, property, the roles of church and state, differing views on marriage and the family, and many other topics. At other meetings we continued to work through the various aspects of Hutterianism that were still a question for us.

Often, as in the earlier years of our life together, we completely forgot the time. If a good discussion with guests developed at lunch or dinner, it could happen that the meal continued for hours. At times these lengthy communal exchanges conflicted with our work, but that did not matter. We wanted everyone to join in the experience. After all, we felt it was these meetings more than anything else that kept us centered on the very reasons we were living together.

In the midst of this joyful time we also had a frightening experience. Because of the added pressures of buildings going up on three sites at once, we had employed workers from the neighborhood, and every Friday, someone would go to Fulda in our buggy to get money for their wages. On one of these paydays, in October 1931, Hans Zumpe and Arno Martin were driving home through the fog with more than 500 marks when two masked men stopped their wagon at gunpoint. Standing in front of the wagon, their guns pointed at our brothers' chests, they demanded, "Give us the money, or we'll shoot!" Hans refused, and crossed his arms over his chest to protect his wallet. In the end, the men didn't shoot, but seized the wallet by force and made off with it. What a terrible shock it was when Arno burst in some time later to tell us what had happened! Yet we were grateful to God, too–both for the fact that our two brothers had not been harmed and that they had not voluntarily handed over the money, which belonged not to them but to the church!

We did not inform the police about the attack. We did, however, invite our neighbors and especially our employed workers to a meeting to tell them what had happened, and asked them that if they ever found out anything about it, they might aid us in seeing that the money was returned. (Despite this the theft was never solved.)

Many years later, in a letter the District Administrator von Gagern wrote me for what would have been Eberhard's seventieth birthday, he mentioned this incident: "I have often admired the consistency of the Bruderhof members in their Christian attitude. For example, two brothers who were carrying the week's pay for their workers–one of them a giant with the strength of a bear–were attacked in the woods by masked figures. Remembering the words of the Savior, they did not defend themselves, but let themselves be robbed."

From October on, Else's health went downhill, and by the end of the year she was so close to death that we knew she would not last much longer. On January 11, 1932, she died–my dear sister, my steadfast friend, my playmate and companion from childhood on.

One year after her death I wrote these lines:

…Why are my longings so earthly
that in my thoughts I seek you
at your place of work, in your devotions,
in the dress you wore when you were here,
when you were still here among us?
How often I am lost in thought
and think: she must come back! Or
waking and dreaming, look with longing,
expecting your return!
There is such pain within me, knowing
that never again am I
to see you as you were…
your loyal face, your eyes warm with love.
And yet your answer comes to me —
as from another world:
"Why do you seek the living here,
Why seek among the dead?"

Eternity means fulfillment,
fulfillment of life, of work, of time.
The words of John come to my mind:
"There shall be no more sorrow,
no separation shall there be,
for the first life, it is over!"
And thus I ask, as bound with you,
you who have gone before us:
Lord, come thou soon and bring thy rule;
unite all who are given thee,
unite us in the Body of Christ,
dwelling of divine promise!

It is more than thirty years ago that Else left us. But her witness to
the powers of eternity is still alive in my memory, and the bond I feel
with her and others who have gone on remains strong. Else was with
us even before the start of our community—from the time of our
awakening in 1907—and she was always one of our closest helpers
and co-fighters. She was loved by old and young. There was something of the spirit of St. Francis in her: in spite of her many tasks

and her devotion to her work, she always had time for the needs of others, and not only those within our own ranks. Her trips in the neighborhood and farther afield to beg for help were never without results. Who could resist this person, so frail in body, but so aflame with enthusiasm and love?

A circular letter sent by Eberhard to our friends in June 1932 says much about Else's last illness that I would like to say, and so I include it here:

> The death of Jesus Christ and the death of the martyrs of old were constantly before the eyes of our dying sister, so that she had to testify, "Nothing greater could have happened than the death of Christ. That is the greatest thing, and in it God's mercy shows itself, mercy in judgment." Else was so deeply gripped by her longing for Jesus and for the kingdom of heaven that she said over and over: "The Spirit and the bride speak: Come! Amen, yes, come, Lord Jesus. The powers of eternity are very near. I am the same weak person I have always been; that has not changed. But Christ's nearness is stronger than ever, so that I am quite far from what happens here and now, and quite close to what is happening there, in heaven. And yet I am also close to God's present history, but it is as if I was looking at it from another star. For myself, I cannot think or wish for anything earthly." One of her very last requests was, "Lift me up; help me to hold my head up."
>
> On January 1, 1932, she said, "This new year will be a very special one, a year of great struggles and of great building up. But there is no life here on earth without struggle. The new life must come through death."
>
> Another time she said, "Eternity is something one cannot understand or grasp. Eternity has always been, will always be. Eternity is very close to me, and its powers are coming to me from God. The greatest thing in God is his mercy. It is so wonderful! And it is wonderful to live in brotherhood. The love and faithfulness of our brotherhood is a miracle. It is incredible that such a thing is possible. How much I love them all! And how dear they all are. A strengthening in mind and spirit must come to the young. In the struggle against themselves they must be set free from all unclarities and all touchiness, giving their strength in steady work. I see clearly that the Bruderhof will grow very large,

and I am glad that I was allowed to be part of the small beginning. Its influence on the whole world will be important, also through mission. I will experience this with you from eternity and will surely be able to help a little too. As often as the spirit of the church unites you and strengthens you for the work, I will be with you. For in the Holy Spirit the whole church is among you. The Holy Spirit brings the Jerusalem above down to you.

"I am so very thankful for the gift of unity. Unity in the Spirit and in the things of the Spirit – that is what endures. Everything we do may express that unity, but it is only an expression. Unity itself is different and greater than all outward expressions. If it is to endure, it must be built only on the Spirit. The expression perishes, but the unity endures.

"It is a wonderful thing to adore God. I should like to worship him always. God is so good, so very good." She turned toward the window and asked, "Are the stars shining? That is where I will be taken. I would so much like to be with the prophets, the apostles, and the martyrs, but probably I will first be with the little children. I have only one wish, that Christ himself may come to fetch me. He is always close to me now. Sometimes I would like to ask God to let me go to sleep, dreaming and without the pains of death, and wake up in eternity. But that would be presumptuous."

In the midst of the worst pain and torment she could cry out, "It is so wonderful; I am so happy, and here in the church it is so wonderful. The life of brotherhood is something wonderful. How I rejoice in the building up. A great time is coming this year, but it will come through struggle and strife. When things are difficult, you must hold to the faith. Always remember that God is the victor in the end. Life is a struggle. In dying this struggle becomes strongest. In life people often don't notice this struggle at all, and so they don't take it seriously."

Another time she told our children: "I am thinking about the ship on which your father Eberhard traveled to America. He wrote then, 'Let us pray that it will be a good landing in God's own land.' And here is the Rhön, the land where our Bruderhof is. Here I will embark to travel to another land, to the most beautiful land there is. I see a long procession full of light. There they are, all of them, and they call to me, 'Come with us!' But Christ is not in front of them or behind them; he is with me. I have fought a great fight."

Else von Hollander, 1931.

Once when Else was looking out of the window with wide-open eyes, someone asked her, "Do you see anyone?" She answered, "No. But I must be on the watch to see when it is coming. Over and over I experience the words from Revelation: The Spirit and the Bride say, 'Come!'"

Often she would gaze into the distance and say several times, quite softly, "Lord, come soon! It is so beautiful to see the day dawning. What will it be like, then, when the eternal morning dawns?"

In the night she sometimes awoke, opened her eyes wide and put her hands together in prayer. Once she said, "I feel as though I were standing between time and eternity, as though I were connecting you with eternity. I need Jesus more than ever, if only he would come soon to get me. When I have to depart, do not part from me! Now sing and be joyful."

In her last days she recalled having seen a remarkable vision of light. On the earth below she saw a great smoky fire, which was not clear or bright, and she felt an oppressive fear that this fire would destroy everything. But suddenly in the middle of this dark-red, smoky fire a tiny, pure white flame sprang up, and this pure flame gave her comfort. Then she watched this small flame spread further and further, and from heaven above came a great, pure, bright flame of light, which united with the small white flame. And straight away, a great city was built out of this pure light. The smoky, sooty fire receded more and more. In the end, the city of light was so bright that the walls of the city were no longer visible. It had become all sun—one single, great, completely white and pure light. Such was her faith in the church that shines out, and the coming down of the Spirit upon the church to build the city on the hill.

Yes, the last months of Else's life challenged all of us like nothing we had experienced before. Often it seemed she had already left us, only to come back again. One time, on awakening from a deep sleep, she said, "The life there is so much more alive than here!" When we asked her what she wished for most of all, she said only, "To have more love!" Not for more days on earth or for relief from her suffering—all she desired was a greater love for others.

On January 11, 1932, after enduring one last long, difficult night, she drew her final breath. Gathering around her bed we could only sing, "Now thank we all our God!" Else had conquered.

10

Before the Storm

Life went on, for we felt Else would not have wanted us to hold up anything because of her. She had even asked us not to let her death interfere with plans for the upcoming weddings of Fritz Kleiner and Martha Braun, Arno Martin and Ruth von Hollander (my sister Olga's adopted daughter). These we celebrated on January 24.

In March, Eberhard and Adolf Braun attended a conference of religious socialists in Bad Boll, Württemberg. This was the place where Johann Christoph Blumhardt and his son, Christoph Friedrich Blumhardt, had worked for over seventy years. Eberhard shared his impressions of the trip in a meeting after he returned, on April 3, 1932:

> The son, Christoph Friedrich, is still remembered vividly today, and a few still remember the father, Johann Christoph. We were glad to find that this memory is a living force today.
>
> Johann Christoph Blumhardt came from the mission school in Basel and from traditional pietist circles into a parish rife with unbelief and superstition. He had a great love for the people and faithfully visited them in their homes, concerning himself with each one personally. Yet thanks to his background he had a broad view of the whole world.
>
> His vision became even broader when he came into tremendous conflict with unbelief. He saw clearly that, if Jesus won victories in his parish, they must have significance for more than Möttlingen and its little congregation alone. In the freeing of Gottliebin Dittus, a possessed woman, forces of darkness were conquered; now, Blumhardt felt, he must go on to fight for the kingdom of God in every corner of the world, so that light might conquer the darkness…
>
> Among the pietists of Württemberg a strong and deep direction had developed that contrasted sharply with the more

Bad Boll, the former spa near Stuttgart made famous by the Blumhardts.

superficial evangelical movement. Thanks to the influence of eighteenth-century theologians, pietism in those days was not nearly so subjective as the pietism of today. But it was soon clear to Blumhardt that he had to take an even broader view. People were healed, devils were driven out, and emotional illnesses were cured. Blumhardt's convictions differed from popular church teachings so much that eventually he had to leave Möttlingen.

Thus Blumhardt came to Bad Boll with his wife and children. He also brought along Gottliebin Dittus, her sister and two brothers, and a certain Theodor Brodersen, who later married Gottliebin. Little by little a small community of fifty people, including children, was formed, living and working together.

Friends told us that both father Blumhardt and his son were modest, almost secretive, about their practice of asking for healing through the laying on of hands. They would have nothing to do with any kind of magic or sorcery. Just as the outward symbol of baptism achieves nothing unless the new birth has already taken place in the heart, so it is, they felt, with the healing of sickness. Not even the least psychosomatic influences should be tolerated…the last thing they wanted was the establishment of a prayer-healing institution.

Johann Christoph Blumhardt had several sons, and two were especially outstanding: Christoph and Theophil. People assumed that Theophil would be his father's successor, but in the end it was Christoph who took over his father's work...

Gradually Christoph broke away from the organized church, from pietism, and from the language of his father...He sought to discern the places *in the world* where God wanted to reveal his kingdom of justice, his victory over evil spirits, and felt that "nothing can be expected from pious people." And so he looked among the common folk – the peasants and factory workers – to find signs of Jesus' victory.

Though he dabbled in politics as a Social Democrat, he was not a politician in the ordinary sense. He was for a time loyal to this party, but the future kingdom of justice and its foreshadowing among the struggles of the working classes excited him far more. There is no question but that he saw God's kingdom as the real answer, the real help...

I do not think he would be very pleased that his sermons and devotions are published and read as widely as they are, and that so many people still flock to Bad Boll. It made him unhappy whenever people tried to imitate him, and he warned them repeatedly neither to overestimate the place, nor his work, nor his own person. Sadly, his warning seems to have gone unheeded. Yet the true significance of his work as I see it has never been truly recognized...

As none of Christoph Blumhardt's sons became his successor, the Moravian Brethren took over the administration of Bad Boll [after his death in 1919], and the present housefather is endeavoring to continue faithfully in his spirit.

We heard testimonies from several who knew the son Blumhardt. One, a widow whose husband (a gardener at Bad Boll) had died in an accident, was taken in by the Blumhardts. Later they bought her a boarding

Christoph Blumhardt (1842–1919), taught that the central message of the gospel has less to do with "religion" than with social justice.

house in Freudenstadt...This woman told me a great deal. She was also very glad to hear of our life and she said it reminded her of the witness of Blumhardt.

I also met a man who discovered the theory of relativity before Einstein. The son of a university professor, he was extremely depressive in his youth, and haunted by demons in a frightful way, to the point that he was suicidal. His depressions alternated with periods of exuberance, during which he felt like a demigod, and in the intervals between these two states, he produced his scientific work.

After living for years in this unbearable way, this man came to Bad Boll, where he encountered Jesus and found freedom from his suffering. I saw him myself—he is an old man, now, a doctor of philosophy. He is not so completely healed that you don't notice anything at all, but he is able to work without sedatives. And he is aglow with fire: he read me his entire story, ten closely-written pages, and confided in me as in a father confessor...

Though Christoph Blumhardt distanced himself more and more from the organized church, he did not experience the true unity of a communal church in his own circle, except in rare instances. It was glimpsed, but never attained...All the same, as Leonhard Ragaz points out, Blumhardt was a man who did not live in his own power and authority. It was the fire of Jesus that radiated from him. Here was a man who expected God to intervene in all of life's problems and in every historical event; a man who had the great vision of God's kingdom and yet took pains for, and stood up for, every individual.

Spring came soon after Eberhard's return from his visit to Bad Boll and with it a renewed effort to build up as much as we could. Guests, especially young ones, continued to come. Annemarie Wächter, who had visited us the previous summer, came to stay on the day of Else's death. Students from Tübingen who had heard about us through our son Hardy (who was studying there) came too, among them Susi Gravenhorst (later Fros) and Edith Boecker (who later married Hardy). There were also Gerhard Wiegand, Ria Kiefer (who read about us in the *Deutsche Sonntagspost)*, Marie Eckardt (an elderly deaconess), Hildegard Friedrich (and her mother Elsbeth), August Dyroff, and Josef Stängl, all of whom stayed.

Meeting with guests under the great beech at the Rhön Bruderhof.

Our guests and new members came from the most varied backgrounds. There were Catholics and Protestants and religious youth from every other persuasion, homeless people, and politically conscious people from both the left and the right. As usual, they brought countless ideas and questions – issues we thrashed out with them under the great beech tree at the end of the day.

Sometimes we had quiet gatherings and at other times the most heated discussions. But no matter the tone, we tried to let ourselves be guided by a spirit of constructive common searching. Thankfully, something of Christ and his church would always break through and shed its light on our meeting sooner or later, and when this happened, everything was able to find its proper perspective.

11

Conflict with Hitler's State

By the summer of 1932, the spirit of Nazism was thriving among many in Germany: "It can't go on like this! It is time to put national interest above self-interest! We need a strong leader!" All this sounded fine, but those who saw deeper realized – on account of Hitler's own ominous pronouncements – how dangerous a leader he might be. And yet, was the steadily growing power of the Bolsheviks any better? We could only hope that both threats, National Socialism and Bolshevism, would pass.

It was through a phone call from our son Heinrich, who was studying at an agricultural school in Fulda, that we first heard the news: Hitler had been appointed Chancellor of the German Reich, and had already taken office. The news came as a surprise to almost everyone, but to those who had a presentiment of what lay ahead, it was an especially great shock.

When new decrees and legislative changes were posted each day, we knew we could expect nothing good. *Gleichschaltung* (the Nazi policy of forced conformity, or "equalization") and the persecution of the Jews were among the first things we heard about. Schools, monasteries, and communities were closed down because they did not want to be "equalized." Germans were expected to greet each other with the salute, *"Heil Hitler,"* and most people complied, assuming that there was no other way. What a pitiful sight it was to see an old lady like our Grandmother Arnold salute someone in this manner! Yet we could understand why people were afraid to say what they really thought about such matters. Anyone who did was labeled a "traitor to the people and enemy of the fatherland."

Every problem, every evil, was blamed on the Jews. At the entrances to many villages, signs were put up saying, "No admittance for dogs and Jews." Soon Germans were no longer allowed to buy in Jewish shops. In some places, for example in Kassel, an area was enclosed with barbed-wire fencing, and anyone caught buying at a Jewish business was denounced and locked inside. Suddenly, the new "science" of race determined everything, and anyone who claimed "Nordic" or "Germanic" ancestry had to prove his "Aryan" bloodline. "Mixed" marriages between Gentiles and Jews were forbidden, and those that already existed were annulled, which caused untold suffering. Many Jews tried to emigrate to other countries, but it was far from simple – indeed, often impossible – to obtain the necessary papers.

Soon columns of Storm Troopers, Black Shirts, and Hitler Youth were parading through even the smallest towns and villages. Their marching songs, especially *Die Fahne hoch!* (Raise high the flag!), were sung everywhere with great enthusiasm. Such aggressive groups came marching through our Rhön Bruderhof too, but they soon realized that we were not willing to participate in their activities. In many a members' meeting we discussed the question: to what extent should we give an opposing witness? We wanted to act openly at all times. We would not be "equalized," that is, accept all the new decrees, and we could not say "Heil Hitler," since we did not believe that *Heil* (salvation) came from him! Naturally this often got us into trouble on the street or in the shops. But how could we cooperate? It was no question to us what spirit Hitler served, and we refused to have anything to do with it.

Already in the first months of 1933 we heard about the closing of schools, particularly progressive ones; about dissidents being deported to concentration camps; about the State's growing opposition to the churches, Catholic as well as Protestant. Before long, free speech was effectively forbidden on all fronts, and every bit of public information had to pass by the censor. Conditions were ripe for disaster. No one knew what was really happening, and the press was no help. Now and then we might see a cryptic notice like, "Another Dangerous Communist Nest Discovered!" but beyond that we knew little.

What were we to do? We all felt the same: we must continue to live for the witness entrusted to us and to speak out. "It will depend on

As if in defiance of increasing oppression by Hitler's State, the Bruderhof proceeded with three new building projects in the summer of 1933.

who holds out the longest," Eberhard said. And so we continued to build. In the spring and summer of 1933 we again had many guests, including some who wanted to stay. Our discussions with them, in particular those concerning National Socialism, were intense, and at times it felt as though every word counted. This was especially true toward the end of the year, when the political climate grew even more repressive. We were not surprised that several who had earlier asked to become members left us, as things grew more dangerous; Eberhard half-jokingly called them our "summer novices." One who did stay was Günther Homann, who worked in our library and archives with great dedication, year after year, until his death.

At Easter 1933 we baptized eighteen new members, most of whom had come the previous year and made clear their intentions to go the way of the cross with us, come what may. Among them were Hans and Margrit Meier, Peter and Anni Mathis, Edith Boecker (later Arnold), Susi Gravenhorst (later Fros), Gertrud Loeffler (later Arnold), and two of our children, Hans-Hermann and Monika. Coming as they did in such a critical time, the baptisms of these new brothers and sisters gave us fresh courage and strength for the way we all had chosen.

In June, despite objections from her parents, we went ahead with the wedding of Marianne Hilbert, a teacher in our school, and Kurt Zimmermann. Tensions with the families of people who came to join us were not unusual, of course, but as Nazism took over the country, the battle lines were drawn more clearly, even among relatives. It had to be all or nothing.

Earlier, after Edith Boecker had joined us, she had been pressured by her parents to come home to Hamburg, at least to say good-bye. Once she arrived, they attempted to talk her out of returning to our community, and when this did not work, they took her travel money and locked her in a second-story bedroom. In the end, Edith escaped: she made a rope with her sheets, let herself down from the window, and made her way back to the Rhön Bruderhof.

Relations with local government authorities were not much better, and Eberhard visited them frequently to clarify our position – namely, that discipleship of Christ, as we understood it, could not be compromised with the demands of National Socialism.

In October, in an effort to lend legitimacy to his government, Hitler ordered a nationwide plebiscite. On October 27 Eberhard went to the authorities in Fulda to explain our attitude to the upcoming plebiscite. An official there told him, "If you don't vote 'yes,' Dr. Arnold, there is only one thing left: concentration camp." Eberhard returned home by taxi. As usual, he walked the last stretch, taking a shortcut over the brow of the hill; this time, however, he slipped on the rain-wet grass, fell, and broke his left leg. Luckily Alfred had gone out to meet him with a lantern, but he was unable to help him to his feet. Running back to the house, he fetched Moni, who came back with him, took one look at the leg, and diagnosed a compound fracture. They had to carry him home on a stretcher.

Eberhard was in great pain, and it was clear the leg had to be operated on as soon as possible, so the next day we drove him back to Fulda, where he underwent surgery. Once back home he was confined to his bed for several weeks.

The plebiscite, which took place on November 12, was not a free election in any sense, but a closely watched show of force. Every person of voting age was compelled to go to the polls, and the authorities made a point of informing us of this. What should we do? After much soul-searching, we decided to go. Rather than refuse to participate—rather than simply say "no" to government, like anarchists—we would use the occasion as an opportunity to witness to our beliefs in a positive way.

Eberhard formulated a short statement declaring that insofar as government was instituted by God, we respected it, but added that our mission was a different one: our task was to live according to the way of Christ, as a corrective to the rest of the world. After discussing this statement in a members' meeting and agreeing to use it, each of us copied it on a piece of gummed paper. Then we went down to Veitsteinbach, the village in whose district we belonged, stuck our statements to our voting slips, and returned home. How surprised we were the next day, when the newspaper reported Hitler's politics had been affirmed at the ballots with a unanimous "yes"!

Four days later, on November 16, our Bruderhof was the target of a surprise raid by the SS, SA, and Gestapo (secret police). About 140 men surrounded the Bruderhof, and no one was permitted to leave his or her room or place of work. Uniformed men stood at every door, and others pushed their way into apartments and searched every room. Books and letters seemed to be of special interest to our visitors, and even personal letters of engaged and married couples were read and ridiculed. Documents from abroad—for example letters from Hardy, who was studying in England under the sponsorship of a Quaker friend—received extra attention.

The secret police searched longest, of course, in our archives, our library, and Eberhard's study, where they expected to find writings and records that proved our "hostility to the state." While the men pushed their way in and out of our rooms, overturning this, and opening that, Eberhard lay on the sofa with his newly operated leg. They probably would have liked to take him away then and there, and throw him in a concentration camp. But what could they do with this sick man? Late that evening a big car drove off loaded with books, writings, and records. What would happen next?

From that day on we were watched even more closely. First, the school superintendent of the district of Kassel, who had formerly been friendly enough, came to administer a test; he wanted to see if our children were receiving sufficient "patriotic" instruction. Ordered to sing the Horst Wessel song, "Raise high the flag," and other well-known nationalistic anthems, they stood open-mouthed, uncomprehending—and failed the test. Then our school was closed (the obvious consequence of the failed inspection), and we were faced with the prospect of having to send our children to a public school in the neighboring village, or hiring a Nazi teacher. On top of this we were informed that any children and young adults whose parents did not live with us would be taken away.

Naturally we had to act fast, so act we did: we decided to whisk all the children we could out of the country. Neighboring Switzerland seemed the best choice for a destination, so we began to work at obtaining a passport and travel permit for each child.

Unfortunately, not all of our children's legal guardians (most of those we had taken in had relatives elsewhere) were willing to help; either they opposed our plan, or supported it but were fearful of getting into trouble. Thus some of the children had to leave us, which we found very hard. Thankfully, several were allowed to stay,

Anxious to avoid the services of a state-appointed Nazi teacher, the Bruderhof whisked away its children to Switzerland. This house in Trogen served as their refuge from January to March 1934.

and in early January 1934 they traveled with Lene Schulz, Annemarie Wächter, and the rest of the children to Switzerland, to a home run by a certain Anna Schmidt.

As for our older children and young adults, it was becoming all but impossible to send them out for schooling. Some broke off their studies, and others who had looked forward to starting were forced to put their plans aside. In many cases, further education now depended on membership in the Nazi youth movement, the *Hitler Jugend,* or the *Bund deutscher Mädchen,* its equivalent for girls. "The future belongs to the youth!" was the slogan.

Other troubles arose too. Visitors who were not members were generally forbidden to stay overnight; if they wanted to stay, we could accept them only if they made a commitment of "membership" for a minimum of six months. Such restrictions were very difficult both for us and our guests, for how were we (or they) supposed to know beforehand who desired to make such a commitment?

Besides all this, our financial situation also grew worse. First, we were told that the twenty-year mortgage on our house (15,000 marks) had to be paid back within two weeks. Second, we were advised that we could no longer sell our turnery, books, or other publications. Third, we were informed that the state subsidies we had been receiving for our school, as well as all support for the orphans we had taken in, would be immediately stopped. Garden produce could have brought in money, if we had had enough to sell; as it was, we needed everything we brought in from the farm for our own household, which now numbered about 180.

With so much weighing on us, we were all the more encouraged by each new addition to our circle—and especially every new baby born to our families. In May 1932, with the birth of Hans and Emy-Margret's daughter Heidi, Eberhard and I had become grandparents; and on December 20, 1933, our wedding anniversary, they welcomed a second child, Hans-Benedikt.

By the early spring of 1934, the home in Switzerland that had taken in our children was asking us to take them back. Eberhard and I were sent to look for a place. Eberhard still had his leg in a walking cast. I saw little hope for a quick recovery, given his continual use of it on our frequent travels. We went first to Liechtenstein, the tiny principality nestled between Switzerland and Austria, and stayed at a village inn in the valley, hoping to get acquainted with the local people. We did not mention our difficulties with the Nazis, but we did say we were looking for a home for children in the vicinity.

While engrossed in conversation at this inn, we overheard someone mention Kurhaus Silum, a summer hotel high on the mountain above the village. Eberhard and I wasted no time in finding the owner. The hotel had stood empty all winter, and the roads and paths were totally covered by snow. It was early March, and we were advised to wait until at least some of the snow had melted. But we could not wait, since the director of the children's home in Switzerland needed the room urgently for a group who had applied previously, and our children had to move out. A friendly farmer from Triesenberg offered to give us a ride up to the hotel in his sleigh, and we asked Adolf Braun, who happened to be in the area on a book-selling trip, to join us.

It was a dangerous trip, for it was very steep and we had to go through deep snow without being able to see the road. On the way our driver told us how many vehicles had already come to grief there! But he was confident he would be able to find the way. And so we traveled up this treacherous mountainside, not without some anxiety, yet knowing we had to find a place for our children. Our driver could not take us all the way to the door of the hotel, so Eberhard had to walk, pulling his cast along behind him through the deep snow-drifts as best he could. At our arrival, we met the owner and went through the house with him. Not everything was perfect, especially the heating. Yet on the whole it was a splendid place, surrounded by the high, snow-covered Alps. A few minutes' walk higher up there was a Swiss cottage, which we could rent in addition to the hotel, and several mountain huts too. Altogether it seemed there would be room for at least a hundred people.

The trip back down the mountain was as hair-raising as the one up had been, for our tracks had almost disappeared under the wind-blown snow. Before we set out, however, we shook hands with the owner on the agreement that we would move in as soon as possible. He named the annual rent and asked for an advance sum of half

The Alm Bruderhof near Triesenberg in the Liechstenstein Alps.

this amount as down payment. For us, who had no money, it was a dizzying sum—about 1,500 francs—and we would have to find it quickly. That night I dreamt we had all tumbled down the mountain.

The next morning Eberhard and I traveled to Chur, where we wanted to visit friends. Because of his bad leg, Eberhard did not go everywhere with me, but stayed in our room. Meanwhile I decided to go to visit Julia Lerchy, a guest at the Rhön Bruderhof the previous summer who was currently hospitalized.

Julia had back trouble and had to lie flat on her back, yet she was very lively and interested in everything I had to tell her. She was shocked to hear of all that had happened to us since she had left in August 1933, but impressed that in spite of all the difficulties, we had gone on building as if we were to live there forever. Julia reminded me of how our enlargements to the dining room the previous summer had meant that Hardy's engagement to Edith Boecker was celebrated in the attic, and we remembered a saying of Martin Luther's: "If I knew that the world were to end tomorrow, I would still plant my apple tree today."

When I took leave of Julia, she asked me to come back in the afternoon with Eberhard. This we did, and during the course of our talk, she told us that she had decided to join the Bruderhof. When we said good-bye, she pressed an envelope into our hands. On opening it outside, we found – to our great joy and gratitude to God – 6,500 francs. Just at this moment, our needs were answered in a way we would have least expected it! Now we could pay the first installment of the rent on our new home in Liechtenstein; we could move the children, buy fuel and food for them, and there would still be more than enough to send on to the hard-pressed Rhön Bruderhof! How ashamed I was of my lack of faith, which had showed itself in my bad dream the night before!

While Eberhard and I went on to visit others in Switzerland, mostly old friends from the religious socialist movement, Adolf helped move the children's group and the sisters with them to the Alm Bruderhof, as we named our new alpine home. It was on this trip that we also visited the Essertines for the first time and met Madame Rossier, the wife of the founder.

At the Essertine community, though we felt the spirit of true brotherhood, we became aware of two important differences between them and us. The first one was celibacy: they believed marriage was a distraction from the all-important task of living for the kingdom, and even couples who were already married did not live together. The second was violence. Whereas we rejected the use of force without exception, they said that in a defensive war, a call to arms was justifiable, and they would not refuse it. What impressed us most was the Essertine attitude to communal work. During lively discussions of an inner nature, they worked weaving baskets, braiding onions, and doing other simple jobs. At the end of our visit, Madame Rossier gave us money and food for our new community.

Before traveling back to Liechtenstein, we went to Peter Mathis's mother, "Nona," who had taken care of our Hans-Hermann during the winter, when he had tuberculosis. He had progressed so well that we could take him with us.

At the new Alm Bruderhof we spent several days with the small but growing circle. New people were coming over the German border almost every day, a few at a time, and we rejoiced with each new arrival. What a wonderful reunion it was – to finally have our children safe from the clutches of the Nazis!

Soon whole families were sent from the Rhön Bruderhof to help, among them the Kleiners and Zimmermanns. Hardy came from England to continue his studies in Zurich, and with him came several people he had met who wanted to try living with us on the basis of the Sermon on the Mount: Arnold and Gladys Mason (a young married couple), Kathleen Hamilton (later Hasenberg), and Winifred Bridgwater (later Dyroff).

It was a very moving time—we had never had guests from England who wanted to join us—and we had one deep-going talk after another with these four. Most of us had more or less forgotten our school English, but Hardy was a good interpreter, and we got on well in spite of the language barrier. Especially memorable for me was our new friends' enthusiasm in turning in their belongings and valuables, which included the Masons' diamond engagement rings.

In August 1934, Hardy and Edith, who had met as students at Tübingen, were married at the Alm Bruderhof. For the wedding ceremony, Eberhard chose "Christ as Head" as his theme, and this message spoke powerfully to all of us. After the wedding, Eberhard and I did not stay long in Liechtenstein, but returned to the Rhön Bruderhof, where we spent the winter of 1934–1935. Hitler's government was growing more repressive by the week, yet we strongly felt we belonged with those who had stayed where the danger was greatest.

On December 20, 1934, we celebrated our silver wedding. A garland of silver thistles hung in the middle of the dining room, adorned with twenty-five tall white candles, and throughout the day we were shown much love by everyone

Wedding procession for Hardy Arnold and Edith Boecker, August 1934.

in the community. Eberhard presented me with a little book he had put together as a gift for me, inscribed "your bridegroom." Little did we know that this would be our last anniversary together.

About this time, Heinrich called us from the Alm Bruderhof, asking our permission to become engaged to Annemarie Wächter. What joy there was that Christmas: Heinrich's engagement, our twenty-fifth anniversary (and my fiftieth birthday as well), and on top of all this, the fact that our children were safely gathered beyond German borders! How grateful we were that God still allowed us such undeserved blessings in a time that held so much darkness and suffering for many!

The new year had barely begun when we were confronted with new questions about the future of our work in Germany. Most significant of these was the issue of Germany's mobilization, and our fears that sooner or later our brothers would be called up for military service.

Children at Kurhaus Silum (the Alm Bruderhof), Liechtenstein, 1934.

We did not have to wait long: on March 16, 1935, Hans Meier, who was traveling in Switzerland, called the Rhön Bruderhof to inform us that the German draft had been reinstated. Within hours, we were able to confirm Hans's news via a source in Fulda: Hitler had ordered mandatory universal conscription, effective immediately. It would only be a matter of days before the first age group would have to register.

That same evening we had a long members' meeting to decide what we should do. Had the hour finally come for us to suffer for our resistance? Or was our task to continue building up a life of community—at the Alm Bruderhof, for instance, where the men were needed for the work? If I remember rightly, there were seventeen young men in our circle who were eligible for the draft, some of them novices, and some of them full members with wives and small children. After a time of silence, and then a prayer in which we asked God for his guidance, we decided to send these men off that same night to the Alm Bruderhof. Money for train tickets was limited, but by midnight they were all gone, traveling by several different routes, and by different means: some by rail, some by bicycle, and some on foot.

The next morning it was eerily quiet. School children we had not had since the previous year, but now there were no young men left—at least no German ones—either. But our loss was the Alm Bruderhof's gain, and before long we began to hear of their arrival, one by one, at the other end. Soon we were rejoicing that all had made it across the border.

At the end of March, we decided to rent a cheap bus so that the young mothers at the Rhön Bruderhof who had been separated from their husbands for weeks, could rejoin them in Liechtenstein. In addition to these mothers and their babies, there were toddlers and three- and four-year-olds, so several others of us went along to care for them.

It was quite an undertaking. The bus, which had hardly any springs, bumped and bounced along all day, and the children, none of them used to traveling, were not easy to pacify. We left early in the morning but had to stop often, and by the time we got to the border it was almost midnight. When we arrived at the crossing, we were refused entry. What a blow! After numerous telephone calls and animated discussions, however, we were finally allowed through.

Happy as we were with the new community in Liechtenstein, we continued to look for a better place to build up outside Germany. For one thing, Silum did not belong to us—we had only rented it—and in any case the land around the house was unsuitable for expansion, for the terrain was extremely steep. As for the Rhön Bruderhof, who knew how much longer our stand against Hitler's racist nationalism would be tolerated?

In spring 1935, the community asked Eberhard to travel to Holland and England to look for a new place and to raise funds for the Alm Bruderhof. Because his leg had still not healed, Hardy, who had made many friends and acquaintances in England during his year of studies there, accompanied him.

In Holland, both Eberhard and Hardy were impressed by the warmth that met them among the people they visited. In England, though their reception was equally heartfelt, Eberhard suffered from considerable strain: partly because of his leg (they had little money, and he often had to walk considerable distances), and partly because so many of the people he met lacked an understanding for the urgency of his pleas for help. Many seemed downright oblivious to developments in Germany.

On Eberhard's return to the continent from England, he traveled first to the Rhön Bruderhof to spend a few days there, but then came on to Liechtenstein. After much persistent begging, he had moved Quaker friends in London to make a donation for a greenhouse (a must for raising vegetables at 5,000 feet, even in summer), and now the little community was finally able to grow more of its food on its own. With the money left over after the purchase of this necessity, we decided to rent a piece of land in the Rhine Valley for further gardening.

Though the soil in our new plot was fertile, the walk down to the river 1,000 meters below us, and back up to the Bruderhof again, was extremely strenuous. Luckily humor often carried the day. I still remember Fritz Kleiner's retort when someone teased him for cutting directly down the steep slope to avoid the endless road with its tortuous twists and turns: "Surely you're not planning to go right down the mountainside, Fritz!" To which he replied, "Well, I don't want to go the way the whole world goes."

After a short visit back to the Rhön Bruderhof for the Whitsun holidays, Eberhard returned to the Alm to find the brotherhood simmering with internal struggles. At stake was the old problem of Hutterianism, in specific the tensions between those who favored the rigidity of its orders and offices and services, and those who longed for the free development of a church led solely by the Spirit. It was an issue that had cropped up before, but at the Alm Bruderhof it had come to the point where some wanted nothing but the old Hutterian teachings, while others wanted only what they felt the Spirit was saying and speaking.

Some, like myself, stood between the two extremes. Conscious of the need for at least some sort of structure to guide a group of weak human beings, I appreciated the order Hutterianism had brought to our life. At the same time I could not accept the thought of a community that did not have room for the Spirit, which had come to us in such a living way again and again over the years. I felt like Eberhard, who had said in a meeting at the time, "If we insist on reading nothing but the old Hutterian teachings" – precious as these were to him – "and force people to accept them, I will have no part in it!"

Yes, we had to fight moralism and legalism over and over; and yet the Spirit still visited us, bringing us new joys and new strength. Two especially happy events that I remember from this time were the wedding of Christian Loeber and Sophie Schwing (the last couple to be married by Eberhard) and the arrival of Hermann Arnold. A nephew of Eberhard, Hermann was so deeply affected by the power of conversion that he resigned from Hitler's SA (Brown Shirts) for reasons of conscience, mailed them his uniform, and joined the Alm Bruderhof. Hermann's father (Eberhard's brother Hermann) had died in World War I, leaving behind a young family. His mother, Käthe, joined us some years later and taught in our school for many years, until her death in 1956.

Just during those difficult weeks of inner struggle in the summer of 1935, Hardy's wife Edith gave birth to her first child, Eberhard Klaus.

Three days later she lay close to death, battling childbed fever and a serious infection. Edith's life hung in the balance, and at times it looked as if it would be extinguished. Day after day, and then week after week, brothers and sisters gathered at the mountain hut where she was being cared for to pray for her.

Edith's baby, not knowing what was happening around him, looked on with innocent eyes. But for the rest of us there was a vital parallel to be drawn between her physical struggle against the powers of illness, and the equally mortal battle of the Alm Bruderhof as a whole as it fought for renewal. Thankfully, the power of life which eventually triumphed in Edith was also victorious over the deadening legalism that threatened our community. That freedom, which the apostle Paul describes so wonderfully in Romans 8, must be sought over and over again. And in every year to come, the fight to win it anew would continue.

12

Eberhard's
Last Struggle

After celebrating Eberhard's fifty-second birthday on July 26, 1935 at the Alm Bruderhof, he and I returned to Germany. For our farewell, the young men and women performed a play they had been rehearsing based on Tolstoy's story, "Where love is, God is."

In the evenings before our departure, Eberhard spent hours looking at the stars through a telescope. Throughout our years together we had often discussed the endless space of the star world and the universe—in comparison to our tiny planet—but in those days toward the end of summer 1935, Eberhard seemed unusually engrossed by this theme. It was not merely scientific or astronomical interest, but a sense of wonder at the greatness of God's creation that stirred us. I especially remember the enthusiasm with which he once showed me Saturn, the planet surrounded by rings of light. Another time we were talking about where loved ones who had gone before us were, and I wondered if Eberhard thought that perhaps he would soon be with them, on one of these stars.

In addition to the star world, the visions of the great prophets, Daniel and Ezekiel (but also of John), consumed us in those days. We felt that there was a close connection between our task as a community in this historical hour, and its significance in the greater scheme of things.

Again and again, Eberhard reminded us of God's great future. It saddened him deeply that we were often too small-minded, too mean and miserable, to see our life in a larger context. It was not that anything "bad" had happened; yet he was distressed by the petty emotionalism into which our brotherhood life so often seemed to sink. Where was our sensitivity, our ear for God's voice? One way Eberhard tried to combat the problem was through trying to open

Eberhard at the Rhön Bruderhof

our eyes to a broader horizon, for instance, by holding talks on the martyrs of earlier centuries, or leading discussions on the current political situation, especially in Nazi Germany. For the most part, people listened, but they were not inwardly receptive.

Eberhard and I made further journeys back and forth between the Bruderhofs that fall, and they were not without danger. People were being stopped, arrested, and dragged off to concentration camps almost daily. Every time we left a community, we did so knowing that we might not reach our planned destination. On top of this Eberhard's leg still caused him considerable pain. In spite of the cast, it was quite crooked, and walking was very difficult for him.

In mid-October 1935, Eberhard and I were both at the Rhön Bruderhof, where we found the same sleepy emotionalism that we had fought so hard with the circle at the Alm. On the surface, things looked fine: the community was functioning, people were working hard, and brothers and sisters generally got on well with each other. But underneath there was little, if any, of the earlier fire that had brought us all together. Instead there were undercurrents of discontent, gossip, frictions over the smallest practical matters, and – what Eberhard abhorred most – a deadening religious complacency. And all this at a critical hour when we were facing serious external threats because of our communal witness! We were reminded of the time Jesus had found his three most beloved disciples asleep.

The ensuing struggle for inner renewal soon developed into a full-blown crisis, and in the end it was clear to all of us that things could not go on any longer as they had. By the agreement of all, we dissolved our brotherhood. We continued to gather for worship meetings, but they were held in silence, and each one used the time to repent – to examine his or her heart and seek anew the spirit of unity and love. It was an hour of bitter earnestness.

To encourage and help us as we fought for a reawakening, the Alm Bruderhof sent Georg and Monika, and Fritz and Martha. They arrived on November 12. Eberhard was only able to see them shortly, as he had to travel to Darmstadt the same day, Dr. Paul Zander, a surgeon and friend we had known since 1907, had offered to examine his leg. Fritz and I accompanied him as he limped along to the edge of the woods; from there, a waiting taxi took him to the train. Little did we know that this was his last farewell – that Eberhard would never see his beloved Bruderhof again.

Difficult days now followed. Already the next day Dr. Zander informed us that he felt a new operation was unavoidable. Eberhard's leg had not healed at all; in fact, it could collapse at any moment. Surgery was scheduled for Saturday, November 16, and I traveled there the day before to be with him.

At the Elisabeth Hospital, I found my husband in bed in a third class ward with three other patients. Dressed in a striped hospital gown, he was busily composing a letter to our son-in-law Hans. I asked him whether he would not like to be in a room by himself; after all, his mother had expressly asked for this and sent the money for it. He replied that he preferred to be among people.

The week after Eberhard's surgery was a hard one. The operation had not gone as well as Dr. Zander had hoped – there were unforeseen complications, and because only local anesthesia was used, Eberhard was conscious throughout: "They sawed, hacked, and then sewed me up," he told me. He spoke little, and when he did it was not about his pain, but about the ongoing struggle at home.

What was uppermost in his mind was the critical importance of our witness – not to ourselves and our achievements, and not even to community, but to Jesus Christ. His life, his words, his death and resurrection, and the outpouring of his Spirit in Jerusalem, with all that followed, was all that mattered. Again and again in those days Eberhard spoke of his love for Christ. He said to me, "When you get home, ask each one, 'Why do you love Christ?'"

At times it seemed he was living in another world. After his death, one of the patients who had shared his room told me, "He was always concerned with God, with the world of the stars and the sun." He was also delirious and confused. Once he asked me to "give the girl sitting over there, the confirmation candidate, a good book to read." When I told him that no one was there, he said he had seen a person in a white dress.

On the Day of Repentance [a Lutheran church holiday], he asked me in a loud voice, "Tell me, have you read anywhere whether Hitler and Goebbels have repented?" I told him I hadn't, and warned him not to say such a thing so loudly, with other people present. At this, he only grew more excited and called out the same question again, even more loudly: "Does anyone here know whether Hitler and Goebbels have repented?"

In the late afternoon of November 21, Frau Zander appeared, looking downcast, and asking to speak alone with my sister Monika, who had joined us at the hospital a few days earlier. Later I found them both in the nurses' room, weeping, and they told me that Eberhard's leg could not be saved: it was completely cold and lifeless. I was dreadfully upset, almost beside myself. Would they really have to amputate above the former fracture, as Dr. Zander proposed? Would Eberhard be able to survive this second operation? Would he learn to walk again? Frau Zander reassured me that his life was not in danger.

Eberhard had not yet been told about the amputation, so when I went to him, I tried to remain very calm. He asked me to read to him something about the coming Advent. I read the first chapter of the Gospel of John: "And the Word was made flesh, and dwelt among us; and we saw his glory." That night he wanted to be alone. Before I went he spoke about the brothers and sisters back at the Rhön Bruderhof, and said, "I will think of you for all eternity!"

As Eberhard was to be sedated very heavily that evening, Monika and I went back to the house where we were staying, though we first asked the night nurse to call us if Eberhard should ask for us, and to let us know if anything special occurred. It was a terrible night: it was as if a black wall loomed in front of me, and I could see nothing at all beyond it. Monika and I read and talked the whole night. We told each other over and over what Dr. Zander had said: that Eberhard's life was not in danger, yet deep down I had the strange feeling that this terrible sacrifice would be demanded.

Very early the next day, November 22, I went to see Eberhard with Monika. He was still asleep when we came. Around 10:30, Dr. Zander came in, examined Eberhard, and gently broke the news to him: the leg could not be saved. Eberhard asked if the operation could not be postponed another twenty-four hours, treating the leg with warming pads and hot air.

Emmy in 1935, the year her husband died.

But Dr. Zander replied, "The surgeon must seize the right time to operate; tomorrow might be too late." Eberhard said, "Then I will submit to it in trust."

Now the fateful operation began, and I sat and waited for it to be over. It was an endless wait: for one thing, the operation took longer than anticipated, and worse, the news that came to me through Moni (who was present) did not sound good. How I longed for the presence of our sons – Hardy, Heinrich, and Hans-Hermann! But they could not possibly risk coming back into Germany; they would have been conscripted immediately, if not imprisoned for evading the draft. Thankfully Emy-Margret and Hans were on the way.

By the time the amputation was completed, Hans and Emy-Margret had arrived, but they were not able to speak with him, for he was still asleep. He never regained consciousness. As we stood around his bed, however, we sensed that he was somehow with us. When we sang – "Thee will I love, my strength, my tower," "Jesus is victorious king," "Yield now, sin and evil deed," and other songs he loved – tears ran down his face.

At four o'clock in the afternoon, he passed away peacefully—his task, his mission finished. It was incomprehensible! We had never dreamt it would happen this way, even though during the last two years I had realized that the time was coming when he would no longer be with us.

Eberhard's burial was held on November 25 at the Rhön Bruderhof, and followed by a special meal in his memory. Immediately after this, Emy-Margret, Monika, and I traveled to the Alm Bruderhof, where Hardy, Heinrich, and Hans-Hermann awaited news of their father's last days.

It is impossible to put into words the meaning of Eberhard's life—either for me as his wife and comrade, or for the many others who knew and loved him. Two years before he died, however, in a meeting with a group of guests, he had spoken about his life of searching, and it seems fitting to quote here what he said:

> I would like to tell about my personal seeking. When I was much younger, groups of people often gathered around me, and I tried by means of Bible studies and talks to lead them to Jesus. But after a while this was no longer enough...I was deeply unhappy. I recognized more and more that a personal concern for the salva-

On November 10, 1935, two days before his departure for Darmstadt, Eberhard and Emmy walked together to the Rhön Bruderhof burial ground. Emmy later recalled, "Eberhard stood looking across the countryside for a long time—it was as if he believed he would never see it again."

tion of souls, no matter how dedicated it might be, did not in itself meet the demands of the life Jesus calls us to...I began to recognize the needs of people in a deeper way: the need of their souls *and* bodies, their material and social wants, their humiliation, exploitation, and enslavement. I recognized the tremendous powers of mammon, discord, hate, and violence, and saw the hard boot of the oppressor upon the neck of the oppressed. If a person has not experienced these things, he might think such words exaggerated – but these are the facts.

Then, from 1913 to 1917, I sought painfully for a deeper understanding of the truth...I felt that I was not fulfilling God's will by approaching people with a purely personal Christianity...

During those years I went through hard struggles: I searched in the ancient writings, in Jesus' Sermon on the Mount and other scriptures, but I also wanted to acquaint myself with the realities of working class life, and I sought to share in the lives of the oppressed as they struggled within the present social order. I wanted to find a way that corresponded to the way of Jesus *and* of Francis of Assisi, not to mention the way of the prophets.

Shortly before the outbreak of the war I wrote to a friend saying that I could not go on like this. I had taken an interest in individuals, preached the gospel, and endeavored in this way to follow Jesus. But I now longed to find a way to *serve* humankind; I wanted to find a life of dedication that would establish a tangible reality – a way of life by which men could recognize the cause for which Jesus died.

The war continued and I saw the condition of men who came back from the front. I will never forget one young man, an officer who came home with both legs shot away. Returning to his fiancée, he hoped to receive the loving care he so badly needed from her, but she informed him that she had become engaged to another man, a healthy one.

Then hunger came to Berlin. Yes, there were still well-to-do "Christian" families who had access to nourishing food and fresh milk, but most people survived on turnips morning, noon, and night. Carts went through the streets bearing the bodies of children who had died of starvation; their bodies were wrapped in newspaper. Who had money for a coffin? In 1917 I saw a horse collapse in the street: the driver was knocked aside by the crowd that instantly gathered around it, and people rushed to cut chunks of meat from the still-warm body to bring home to their families.

Once I visited a poor woman in a dark basement dwelling, where water seeped down the walls. Although she was tubercular, her relatives were living in the same room with her. One could hardly keep the window open; too much dust would have been kicked in by people walking past in the street above. I offered to find this woman a different place to live, but she no longer possessed the will to live: "I'm not going to make a fool of myself. Leave me here; I'll die here where I have lived." Inwardly, she was already a corpse.

After such experiences – and those of the revolutionary times that followed, when the poor traded places with those they had overthrown and occupied huge halls with parquet floors – I realized that the whole situation was unbearable. How could a Christian remain silent on the most pressing social issues: war, injustice, and human suffering?

In the meetings Emmy and I had later had at our home in Berlin, where we met and discussed all these things with our friends, we soon came to feel that Jesus' way must be a practical one: he had shown us a way of life that was comprised of more than a concern for the soul. It was a way that simply said, "If you have two coats, give one to him who has none. Give food to the hungry, and do not turn away your neighbor when he needs to borrow from you. When you are asked for an hour's work, give two. Strive for justice. If you wish to found a family, see that all others who want to found a family are able to do so, too. If you wish for education, work, and satisfying activity, make these possible for other people as well. If you claim that it is your duty to care for your health, then accept this duty on behalf of others too. Treat people in the same way that you would like to be treated by them. That is the wisdom of the law and the prophets. Finally, enter through this narrow gate, for it is the way that leads to the kingdom of God."

When all this became clear to us, we realized that a person can go this way only when he or she becomes as poor as a beggar and takes upon himself, as Jesus did, the burden of every person's need...Only then – when we hungered for justice more than for water and bread, and were persecuted for the sake of this justice –

would our hearts be undivided; only then would our righteousness exceed that of the moralists and theologians. Then we would be filled with the Holy Spirit, and with a new warmth—with the fire that blazes from the vital energy of God.

It was clear to us that the first Christian community in Jerusalem was more than a historical happening: rather, it was here that the Sermon on the Mount came to life. Therefore we felt we could not endure the life we were living any longer, but saw that it was more necessary than ever for us to renounce the last vestiges of privileges and rights and to let ourselves be won for the way of total love...

Jesus made the blind see, the lame walk, and the deaf hear. And he prophesied a kingdom, a rule of God that will overturn every unjust condition in the present order of the world, and make it new. To acknowledge this and to live according to it—this is God's command for the hour.

The Fight Goes On

The days and weeks that followed Eberhard's death are difficult to remember and difficult to write about. All were greatly shaken – especially at the Rhön, but also at the Alm Bruderhof – by his passing, but there were other things we were coping with too. Above all, our struggling brotherhood needed to be restored and newly founded.

Over many years, but in particular during the last difficult ones before Eberhard's death, guests had warned us that a life like ours would last only as long as its founders were still living. After the first members died, they said, the whole thing would collapse, for without their conviction and enthusiasm, there would be no way to stave off decline. In answer to this we had always said that although such a theory might hold true for a human organization, it could not be so for a community established and guided by the power of the Spirit. Now this had to be proved.

Certainly, our communal beginning at Sannerz was something we had longed for, but it was never a matter of human charisma or idealism. The Spirit called it into life. Our community came into being out of desperation and yearning, out of bloodshed and confusion. It arose in an atmosphere in which people had come to the end of all they knew – the loss of house, home, and livelihood, and the bankruptcy of earlier answers and ideals. At that time the question had come from all sides, "What shall we do?" And now, after Eberhard's sudden death, we had to answer this question again.

At the Rhön Bruderhof, a hard fight against sin continued to be waged, especially where it had been let in through emotionalism, which is always a disturbance in a community. But there was also disloyalty and cowardice, gossip, cliquish friendships, self-pity, excessive sympathy for some, and insufficient compassion for others. It is

still hard for me to understand how these things could have gained
so much ground among us in a time when our witness against the
spirit of Hitler and his religion of hatred was so sorely needed. And
how could it be, that just in this critical hour, Eberhard, my husband
and friend, counselor, and spiritual guide, had left us forever?

The fight was a call to action and to unity. For myself and my children, who were especially hard-hit, it was a help, for it redirected our
thoughts away from our grief and toward others. But who was not
especially affected? What about all the children we had taken in and
brought up in our family over the years; and what about the many
others, including young men and women for whom Eberhard had
been a father?

The challenge was for everyone. Each individual had to clarify
his or her position and address Eberhard's last question, "Why do
you love Christ?" Some did not come through the struggle so easily.
As for the rest of us, I am sure a better, more conciliatory way could
have been found. I feel this especially for myself: only later did I see
that the same sins recognized by others had to be fought in my own
heart too.

In spite of all this, and in spite of the immense loss we suffered
through Eberhard's death, we felt as determined as ever to continue
building up. At the Rhön Bruderhof (and everywhere else in
Germany), things were getting more difficult all the time. Problems
also came up at the Alm Bruderhof, even though there most of our
neighbors were friendly. Then Liechtenstein announced that it was
no longer ready to harbor foreigners if other countries—for instance,
Germany—claimed them for military service. On top of this, the
German passports of several brothers and sisters (including Hardy
and Heinrich) were expiring and had to be renewed.

Luckily, it was just at this time—spring 1936—that a solution for
many of these troubles came: suitable land for a community was
found in England. The property was named the Cotswold Bruderhof,
and by June, several families had already moved there from the Alm
Bruderhof.

Heinrich and Annemarie, who had married in March, moved to
England at the end of their honeymoon, and some time later Hardy
and Edith and their little boy followed them.

Traveling was not without dangers and unexpected delays. For example, when Hardy went to the German consulate in Zurich to pick up his passport and refused to return the greeting, "Heil Hitler," the attending official, who had already handed him his papers, insisted on taking them back. Edna Percival (later Jory), a new English member, attempted to get them for him but did not succeed. She was told that the owner of the papers had to receive them in person. Thankfully everything turned out well in the end: Bruderhof members in England contacted the British Home Office and applied for Hardy and his family be permitted into the country without their papers. The request was approved.

Others were not so fortunate. Werner Friedemann, a German member who was trying to raise money for the Alm Bruderhof by selling books in Switzerland, was caught without a police permit, arrested, and jailed. After several days Werner was released, but could no longer come home to Liechtenstein: in the time since he had left, his age group had been called up.

England was the only safe destination, so with great pains the necessary fare was rustled together. We then took him to the Zurich airport, got him on his plane, and said farewell. Imagine our horror, the next day, when we were informed by phone that he had been denied entrance to England and returned to Zurich. What were we to do? Even outside Germany we were being closely watched, and at that time it often happened that dissenting citizens who had fled the country were forced back over the border, apprehended, and thrown into the concentration camps, never to be heard of again. We knew we had to be both daring and cautious.

In the end, the problem of getting our young Germans to England was solved by forming a wandering musical troupe, complete with lutes, guitars, fiddles, and flutes, and led by a Swiss member, Hans Meier. Skirting Germany, the group traveled through Switzerland and made their way west toward France without incident. Crossing the Swiss-French border proved to be easy: it was late at night, and the sleepy young guard at the customs house glanced briefly at Hans's Swiss passport, nodded, and let the entire troupe through! Later, taking a train north to the English Channel, there was some worry when the police asked why none of the group's passports contained mention of their entry into France. But their good luck continued, and soon everyone was safely in England.

The story of how the Cotswold Bruderhof was begun is a remarkable one. As I have told earlier, our English friends had helped us in many ways, especially with their gift of money for a greenhouse at the Alm Bruderhof. Now, in this time of new anxieties, they offered to take in our members of military age. Unfortunately the offer allowed for no community, but only for individual accommodations in various locations, and we had to decline. Our hearts were set on the continued expansion of our brotherly life, and that was why we had decided to send our young men out of Germany – not to save the skin of this or that individual.

In the end we had no choice but to go looking for a place ourselves. A car was rented, and several brothers went out to look for a suitable farm to rent or buy. They had no money, nor had the government granted us permission to stay in England as foreigners! But they set out full of courage and faith that God would show them the way. After looking at a number of possibilities, they found a farm near Ashton Keynes, Wiltshire. The owner was ready to lease it to us, though he required a large down payment right away.

The Cotswold Bruderhof in Wiltshire, England, founded in 1936.

Meanwhile the number of young men arriving from Germany and Liechtenstein had grown so fast that there was no other alternative but to move in, before so much as a penny had been paid. Naturally the owner of the farm was more than a little astonished to find out about this, and told us, "This is not usually done in England." Nor in other countries, I think.

Money for the down payment was raised quickly, though not without persistent begging. Heinrich and several other brothers were sent out for this, and they went all over England to relatives, friends, and acquaintances—anyone who might help us. Heinrich even approached people who had never heard of us, telling them our story of persecution in Germany and our flight to England. Amazingly, many donated funds. A furniture company in Bristol even handed over two hundred pounds on Heinrich's word alone, with little further proof. (They also helped us later by giving us beds, which we took to South America when war forced us out of England in 1940.) Others also gave generously.

While all this was happening in England, we struggled to keep the Alm and Rhön Bruderhofs afloat. Staffing was short at both communities, money was continually a problem, and the political situation weighed on us like the air before a storm. During the spring and summer of 1936 especially, we survived on next to nothing, and sometimes it felt that we made it through the day only by a miracle.

All the same, we refused to retreat into our shells. If anything, we felt a renewed urgency to witness publicly to the life of justice and love and brotherhood that had been entrusted to us, and to call others to join us on the way. Eberhard had admonished us precisely in this regard some months before his death, saying, "When we are no longer able to be there for *all* people—when we can no longer concern ourselves with the need and suffering of the whole world—our communal life no longer has any right to exist."

In late June 1936, Hans Zumpe and I were sent to attend a Mennonite peace conference in Amsterdam, Holland, which Eberhard and I had planned to attend. We were surprised by how few

German Mennonites attended the conference, and shocked to learn how quickly they had become influenced by the spirit of the times. Indeed, from all Germany there was only one busload of serious conscientious objectors, and most of the passengers were Americans. (It was at this conference that we first met Orie Miller of the Mennonite Central Committee. A loyal friend for the rest of his life, he helped us resettle in Paraguay when we were forced to leave England during the Second World War.)

After the conference, Hans returned directly to Germany,

Emmy at the Cotswold Bruderhof, 1936.

while I traveled to England to visit the Cotswold Bruderhof. (As an indication of how closely we were spied on, it is interesting that though we had taken great pains to keep our British address a secret, a German official in Kassel surprised Hans some weeks later by showing him the location of our new community on a map of England!)

In comparison to the great poverty at the Rhön and Alm Bruderhofs, where even most basic necessities were hard to come by, England seemed rather comfortable to me, though there too (like everywhere else) the establishment of community did not come without struggle. But what enthusiasm there was in building up the new life, and what energy among the young brothers and sisters who made up the circle there! At the end of the summer, I returned once more to Liechtenstein, where I stayed the next several months.

Shortly before Christmas I made what was to be my last visit to the Rhön. The little circle there was struggling bravely – an island of opposition in a sea of support for Hitler, but the atmosphere was uncomfortably heavy. Neighbors and local officials watched every coming and going, every move, and the brothers and sisters who lived there grew increasingly suspicious that new troubles were afoot.

On April 14, 1937, we received an unexpected phone call informing us that the Rhön Bruderhof had been surrounded by the Nazi secret police, the property was to be confiscated, and the entire community had twenty-four hours to leave the country (this was later extended to forty-eight hours on account of a flu epidemic among the children). The reason was clear: our way of life was regarded as a dangerous affront to the power of the state, and we were therefore *unerwünscht* ("undesired") in Germany. For several years we had reckoned that something like this would happen; even so it was a great shock for us all when it finally came about, and so suddenly.

It was surely a good thing that two Hutterite brothers–David Hofer of James Valley, Manitoba, and Michael Waldner of Bonhomme, South Dakota–happened to be at the Rhön Bruderhof on the day of the raid. They had traveled from North America some months before, arriving at the Cotswold Bruderhof in February and continuing on to Europe some time later. Without their presence as foreigners, who knows what might have happened? Since I was not there at the dissolution of the Rhön Bruderhof, I would like to describe it by quoting from David Hofer's diary; it includes his first-hand impressions of the fateful day.

April 14, 1937
About 10:00 a.m. Michael Waldner and I were in Eberhard Arnold's room writing letters, when Hans Meier opened the door and said, "Brothers, prepare yourselves, for I have just come from the top of the hill, where I saw a large number of police in the woods. They may come to the Bruderhof, but they cannot do anything to you." Then he closed the door and went to his office to tidy up. Thereupon I went to the window and saw uniformed men hurrying down the hill. I went down to see what would happen.

There were already twenty-five policemen standing at the door. "Where is Hans Meier?" one shouted at me. I answered quite simply, "Doubtless in the house." "Call him out here!" was the next order. As I went to Hans Meier's room he met me and then introduced himself quite calmly and fearlessly to the police. The chief officer read Hans Meier the order: "I inform you herewith that the Rhön Bruderhof is now dissolved by the state and must exist no longer. From now on it is to be called 'Sparhof,' and as you are leader of this Bruderhof, I demand all books and keys from you. I inform you also that within twenty-four hours everyone must leave the place!" Then he went straight to the office with Hans Meier. The other police surrounded the whole Bruderhof and drove all brothers and sisters, young and old, into the dining room. There they were guarded by two policemen, and no one was allowed either out or in, while the others searched every room and took whatever they wanted. At last they came to our room, where we were waiting. They ordered us to join the brothers in the dining room. We went down quite calmly to the brothers and sisters, and found them perplexed and discouraged. We encouraged them and told them not to despair.

Then two officials came in. One carried a typewriter, the other a bundle of papers. They sat down and called each one by name, and each had to answer what he was asked and then sign the filled-in form. The form was only a proclamation regarding registration for assembly—we examined it carefully before signing. In the meantime, through the window we saw them searching all the rooms and carrying all that they wanted to their cars. When I saw that they were soon getting to our room, I wanted to go there. But at the door I was stopped and told to stay in the dining room. I said, "I want to go to my room. We are foreigners and do not want our things searched and carried off." He said he was not allowed to let anyone out. "If you want to go out, you must get written permission from our chief officer and bring it to me." I asked, "Where is he?" He said, "Upstairs in the office." I went upstairs and applied to the chief officer (who was occupied with Hans Meier) for leave to go to my room, which he granted me.

Then I called Michael Waldner and we went to our room together. Before long, they came and began to search. We told them that we were foreigners, even of German extraction, and did not want to have our things searched. They asked us what we wanted with these people here, where we were from, and what had brought us to these people. We told them, "These people are our brothers in the faith, to whom we have sent much help from America to build up this Bruderhof. Therefore we take a great interest in what is happening here and what will happen to them." We saw at once that our presence was no pleasure to them, and that we were in their way. We asked them to allow us to stay for a few days. They refused and said that that was no concern of theirs. By now all the brothers and sisters had signed the forms. It was 3:00 p.m. by the time they had finished, and only then were they allowed to have some food. Our food, however, had already been brought to us and we had already eaten.

Meanwhile the police stood outside the dining room and talked together. I went out to them and talked with them about what was happening. I told them that what we had experienced here today was quite uncalled-for, and that we had not expected such a thing of Germany. I thought they would have treated their citizens and peasants better than what we had to see and experience today. I told them they were worse than the Americans were. They asked, "How?" I told them that we as Germans were called up in the last war to do military service against Germany. We objected and refused to do it, just as these brothers of ours had done. We asked our government in America to give us the freedom to leave the country, as we could not obey it in doing military service. We asked to be allowed to sell all we had and to leave nothing behind – all of which was granted. During the war we were allowed to emigrate to Canada, and this under government protection so that nothing might happen to us.

I asked them why they could not treat this community the same way. They asked, "Why can't you people show your obedience to the government like everybody else?" I told them clearly that we respected the government, but that we could not obey when it demanded something against our conscience. One of them asked me, "To what extent?" I told them that the Word of God tells me to love my neighbor and not kill him, and for this reason I could not follow and obey the government. Then another spoke: "Friend, have you not read that our Savior said, 'I have not come to send peace but the sword,' and that he also told his disciples to buy swords? Why do you not believe these passages of the scriptures?" I told him how I understood these passages. He said my interpretation was wrong, adding, "If the whole world consisted of angels, like all of you, then there would be no need of war, but you know that not all men are like that." "We also do not want war," they insisted. "We only want to make ourselves strong, because everyone fears the strong. If we are weak, they will walk all over us. But if we are strong, they will fear us. That is why we prepare for war, not because we want to fight."

The others thought the brothers and sisters were taking too long to eat and asked, "Do they have a whole ox to devour in there, that they are taking so long about it?" After the meal they ordered the whole community to assemble outside the door. Michael Waldner and I were also ordered to do so, as though they had a proclamation to read. I soon saw, however, that they only wanted to take photographs, so I left the group saying to Michael Waldner, "Come into the house." To them I said, "We do not need that." Then the order was read that the Bruderhof was now dissolved, that no Bruderhof existed anymore in Germany. No one was to take along anything from the farm or the property of the community, or any household goods. After reading this out, they all left the place.

We met for prayer with very troubled and sorrowful hearts. We told God of our need and distress and earnestly prayed to him not to forsake us in this difficult time, but to give us true understanding and wisdom to act according to his will.

After the prayer we considered our situation, and how we could bring it about that the community might remain together. The godless men wanted to scatter the brothers and sisters all over Germany by sending them to their relatives. We also desperately wanted to let the communities in England and Liechtenstein know what was happening here at the Rhön Bruderhof.

So we decided that Arno Martin, the steward of the Alm Bruderhof who was just about to return there, should inform Hans Zumpe and the community in England as soon as he had crossed the German border. But how were we to send anyone? The police had robbed us of all our money – over 400 marks. There was not a penny in the house. They had been robbed of everything, including keys and books, and all communal rooms were locked. So we gave the brothers and sisters our traveling money, and Hans

Meier and I went with Arno Martin to Schlüchtern, arriving at midnight. There we saw him off with the sad news, which he was to bring to the Cotswold Bruderhof and to Liechtenstein.

Hans Meier and I returned to the community with heavy hearts, and found them all still up. We went to bed but slept little.

April 15, 1937
Arose once more in good health, for which we give thanks to God. Also had some breakfast. After breakfast Hans Meier came in great haste and told us that a gentleman from Fulda was in the court-yard with his car, demanding that the board of directors go with him to Fulda to settle some trifling matters. After that they would be able to return. This news was an unhappy surprise for me. I did not believe what the gentleman from Fulda said. I said to Michael Waldner, "Do you believe that these brothers will be back by midday, as he promises?" Michael Waldner said, "I don't know; he promises it." I said, "We shall see when the time comes." Hans Meier, Hannes Boller, and Karl Keiderling got ready and left.

The whole community waited anxiously, but at twelve o'clock no brothers came. Two o'clock came, and four o'clock – still the brothers did not come. Then Michael Waldner and I went up the hill where they would arrive. We saw a car coming and recognized it at once as the car that took the brothers away. A man got out and came to us. I asked, "Where are the brothers?" "They have not come," was the answer. Immediately he ordered me to call the whole community together. First he read us the order to leave the place within twenty-four hours.

The officers also brought letters from the three brothers to their wives – Margrit, Else, and Irmgard – telling them that they had been imprisoned, but encouraging their wives and children, and all in the community, to trust in God's leading and leave the next day as ordered.

At the request of the three brothers in Fulda, the whole community was to be permitted to leave together, and the government was willing to let us take our five brothers of military age with us. So everyone signed a document saying that they would leave the Bruderhof and travel to the other communities. However, as several brothers and sisters had no passports, and as we wanted to speak with the brothers in prison regarding their families, I asked the chief officer for a written note permitting me to see the brothers in Fulda. He agreed, and when everything was settled, they left.

We gathered together for prayer and comforted ourselves with the word of God. I read Psalm 3 as an encouragement, and thanked God that he had so changed and directed matters that the brothers and sisters could join the other communities. We prayed fervently to God not to forsake us in this great trouble, but to send his guardian angels to watch over and protect us.

After the prayer, preparations were made for the journey. We advised the brothers and sisters to get as much food as they could from the pantry as provision for the journey. For it was their store of food, and they should take what they needed.

At five o'clock the next morning, six of our brothers and sisters left to go to Fulda for passports. I went with them to visit the brothers in prison. I brought them the news that at six that evening, the whole community would leave Germany, with their wives and children. The brothers were grateful that the community was caring so faithfully for their families. As well as I could, I encouraged the imprisoned brothers to be patient—our gracious God would not forsake them. Then I took leave of the brothers with a heavy heart and went back to the office where the others were, to get the passports as quickly as possible and to arrange for tickets. When it was settled, we returned home.

We arrived safely at the Bruderhof at 4:00 p.m. and found Michael Waldner and all the brothers and sisters busy packing and preparing for the journey. It was very hard for the brothers and sisters to leave the results of the sweat of their brows and depart empty-handed. At 5:00 p.m. we had a bite to eat, and then met again for prayer—for the last time at the Rhön Bruderhof. We prayed to God to protect his church on this journey, which we were about to begin. We trusted in his faithful promise not to forsake us, but through his grace to accompany us and bring us in peace to his children in the other communities. God has faithfully helped us all, so that we have come back to the church in good health.

It had rained all day, especially in the afternoon, and we were anxious about several sick children and a sick sister, for we had to go more than a mile over the hills to the trucks, and they might catch cold on the way. When the time came, however, and all were ready to leave, suddenly the sun shone brightly. The rain had stopped and the sun shone down on us. To us this was a wonder and grace of God, and we thanked him in our hearts.

Now the brothers and sisters began to climb the hill with their sick ones, each with a bundle on his or her back. Michael Waldner carried a child on his back. I carried a large bundle for Hans Meier's wife, who had given birth two weeks earlier. We were all laden; everyone's hands and backs were full. With heavy hearts we climbed the hill, stopping several times to look back at the beautiful Rhön Bruderhof, the beloved home we had to leave so suddenly and unexpectedly. Some went to the burial ground to visit the grave of our beloved Eberhard Arnold for the last time.

When we arrived at the appointed place, the cars were already there. When they were loaded, they set off for the station. Michael Waldner, Hella Römer [the Bruderhof bookkeeper, who had been instructed to stay until everything was put in order], and I were the only ones left at the Rhön Bruderhof. We returned to the empty place with sad and deeply perturbed hearts. We went early to bed, but our uneasiness did not let us get much sleep. Next morning we began to tidy the rooms. The picture that met us cannot be described: food was left on the tables, the bedclothes lay in a heap on the beds. In the kindergarten the toys and furniture lay about as the children had left them. In the laundry the clothes lay unwashed, soaking partly in tubs and partly in the boiler. It was a perfect wilderness, enough to make the heart break and the eyes weep. Never had we seen such a sight before...

This is my short account of how the Rhön Bruderhof was dissolved by the German government.

I experienced all this from the Alm Bruderhof: the telephone calls, the worry over the safety of loved ones, and finally their arrivals. First the deported brothers and sisters (including Julia Lerchy, who came on a stretcher because of her bad back) came; they were followed several days later by the two Hutterian brothers and Hella Römer. How we rejoiced to have them all with us!

We were still sick with worry, of course, over the three brothers imprisoned in Germany. In those days of concentration camps and "disappearances," it was only natural to fear the worst. As it was, they were held by the Gestapo for almost ten weeks, and then suddenly released. Because the story is such an amazing one, I would like to include it here.

On June 26, a Saturday, the prison warden appeared without warning and told the three brothers to pack their things immediately and get ready to leave. Not knowing where they were being moved, the brothers were anxious, especially when they were escorted to the prison gate and saw a black car waiting for them. Ordered to get in, they were driven away at high speed. After an hour or so, the driver stopped suddenly in the middle of a forest, told them to get out as quickly as possible, and directed them toward Königstein, a nearby town. Here they were met by Quakers who sent them from one connection to the next until they got to the Dutch border, which they reached at night.

Crossing into Holland through an unknown forest in the middle of the night proved to be a gamble. On the first attempt the brothers lost their way and came out on the German side, where a German guard stopped them. Incredibly, they were able to convince him that friends on the other side of the border expected them, and he not only let them across but also showed them the way to the nearest Dutch village. It was from here that they made their way to England.

Reunion of three Bruderhof members with their wives and others in England, July 1937, after two months in a Nazi prison.

Given the happenings of those last two years at the Rhön Bruder-hof—in particular the loss of my husband, our harassment by the State, and finally the loss of everything we had, one might ask how it was possible for us to go on. After all that we had experienced in seventeen years of living together in Germany—after all that we had struggled for, fought through, and won—what had we gained?

Looking back, I can only say that we did not feel so much disheartened as filled with deep thankfulness. Yes, the first wonderful chapters of our community life were closed in a way we might never have expected, but at the same time, new horizons were opened to us, and we looked forward to the future with eagerness and joy.

In the past, whenever we had put aside our fears and trusted in God, he had led us step by step, and we were certain he would guide us in the future as well. Hardships and struggles, human failings and attacks from without and within—these would always be a part of the path we had chosen. But how could we let such things stop us from continuing on the way? We had heard the call clearly, and there was no choice but to follow it.

Eberhard says it much better than I could, and so I would like to close this book with his words. They come from "Why We Live in Community," a statement he wrote at Sannerz in 1925:

> In the life of a community, several decisive questions need to be confronted again and again: How are we called? To what are we called? Will we follow the call? Only a few are called. Yet those who are—a small, battle-tried band, who must sacrifice themselves again and again—will hold firmly for the rest of their lives to the common task shown them by God. They will be ready to sacrifice life itself for the sake of unity...
>
> Community life is like martyrdom by fire: it means daily readi-ness to relinquish all our power, all our rights, all the claims we commonly make on life and assume to be justified. In the symbol of fire the individual logs burn away so that, united, its glowing flames send out warmth and light again and again into the land...
>
> People tear themselves away from home, parents, and career for the sake of marriage; for the sake of wife and child they risk their lives. In the same way it is necessary to break away and sacri-fice everything for the sake of our calling to this way. Our witness

to voluntary community of goods and work, to a life of peace and love, will have meaning only when we throw our entire life and livelihood into it...

Our life, then, is a venture dared again and again. Yet we are not the driving force in this—it is we who have been driven and who must be urged on...Efforts to organize community in a human way can only result in ugly, lifeless caricatures. Only when we are empty and open to the Living One—to the Spirit—can he bring about the same life among us as he did among the early Christians. The Spirit is joy in the Living One, joy in God as the only real life; it is joy in all people, because they have life from God. The Spirit drives us to all people and brings us joy in living and working for one another, for it is the spirit of creativity and love.

Postscript

After the expulsion of the Bruderhof from Nazi Germany and the emigration of its members to England, the movement grew by leaps and bounds. Young British war-resisters and left-leaning progressives disillusioned by conventional religion seemed especially attracted, and by 1940 the community had more than doubled in size.

The same year, however, tensions with neighbors who feared the presence of "enemy" aliens in the country forced another emigration – this time across submarine-infested seas, to South America. There, in the Paraguayan wilderness, "Primavera" (Spanish for spring) was founded in 1940, and remained the center of Bruderhof activity for the next twenty years.

Life in Paraguay was hard, and not only because of the harsh climate, subtropical diseases, and primitive living conditions. Aside from these, the community underwent one internal crisis after another – most of them the result of power struggles – and there was a gradual shift "away from Jesus" (as Emmy put it) and toward a principled, legalistic emphasis on community as an end in itself.

In the 1950s, additional Bruderhofs were established in Uruguay, England, Germany, New York, Pennsylvania, and Connecticut. Emmy moved to Woodcrest, the first American one (in Rifton, New York), in 1960. Though seventy-six, she seemed rejuvenated by the influx of young seekers who had flocked to the communities in the post-war years, and she welcomed the fresh wind they brought with them. Whereas at Primavera Emmy felt Eberhard's original dream of a new society had been obscured by all-too-human attempts to preserve the Bruderhof as a structure, at Woodcrest she rejoiced to find new zeal, new spiritual freedom, and a new yearning for the leading of the Spirit.

Always eager to know what was on another person's heart, Emmy loved to talk with guests, young adults, and new members. A great listener, she was sensitive to their questions and struggles, and often had an encouraging word for them. At the same time she did not hesitate to express her conviction that the "first love" – the love of God that had inspired the founding of the community – must be kept alive. "The rule of the Holy Spirit in our life has to be proved over and over."

Though Emmy missed her husband throughout her forty-five years of widowhood, her sense of loss only strengthened her resolve to keep his vision alive. In Primavera this cost her more than a few battles, in particular when Eberhard's witness was criticized and even rejected by members as unviable or unrealistic.

Emmy refused to defend herself or to indulge in self-pity, however, and turned instead to the things that had sustained her through so many years. Aside from the New Testament (with her beloved Gospel of John), there were the Psalms, many of which she knew by heart, and her favorite choral works: Bach's *Saint Matthew's Passion,* Handel's *Messiah,* and Mendelssohn's *Elijah.* Let others misunderstand her – she was determined to hold faithfully to the way of Jesus shown to her and Eberhard from the very beginning of their life together. "In times of struggle, I am strong," she would say, or: "That is our life: a fight, or a celebration!" And she was always forgiving. Once a hurt had been resolved and forgiven, she never referred to it again.

Emmy was no pious matriarch. True, she was a mother to us all – to her own children, grandchildren, and great grandchildren, to the young men and women who flocked to the community in the early years, and to many who joined later, leaving house and home, father and mother, relatives and friends for the sake of Jesus. But there was no hint of smugness in her – no self-serving religiosity, no consciousness of her authority as a co-founder (she hated the term), no awareness of her long experience. Rather it was her modesty and quiet clarity, even in periods of turmoil and confusion, that made her a vital part of the community.

As for her legacy to succeeding generations, Emmy's devotion to the dissemination of her husband's writings is unmatched. In addition to reading through notes and transcripts of the several thousand talks Eberhard gave between 1907 and 1935, she spent years

Emmy at Woodcrest Bruderhof in Rifton, New York, her home from 1960 to her death in 1980.

gathering and sorting his books, essays, articles, and letters, and copying out excerpts she found significant, often in beautiful calligraphy. Several of these collections became books: *Salt and Light, When the Time Was Fulfilled, Love and Marriage in the Spirit,* and *Seeking for the Kingdom of God.*

Emmy took great interest in every new chapter of our communal life, but she was especially happy about the revival of our publishing house in the 1960s. When the first copy of these memoirs (titled *Torches Together*) was presented to her at a festive gathering, she covered her face with her hands in embarrassed pleasure.

Even in her eighties, Emmy participated in as many communal meetings and mealtimes as she could, and whole-heartedly joined in the singing. In her early nineties, however, she told a visitor, "I am ready to leave this world. But each morning when I wake up, I am happy, because I have been given another day to love and to serve." Emmy died at Woodcrest Bruderhof on January 15, 1980, at the age of ninety-five.

For more information about the community described
in this book, visit **www.bruderhof.com**.
We welcome visitors.

Other Titles from Plough

Against the Wind
Eberhard Arnold and the Bruderhof
Markus Baum
A journalist's account of the life of an uncompromising revolutionary for Christ whose witness still lives on.

The Early Christians
In Their Own Words
Eberhard Arnold
A topically arranged collection of primary sources that provides a guide and yardstick for Christians today. This is a book that all students, priests, librarians, and history lovers will want on their shelves.

God's Revolution
Justice, Community, and the Coming Kingdom
Eberhard Arnold
Topically arranged excerpts from the author's talks and writings on the church, community, marriage and family issues, government, and world suffering.

Salt and Light
Living the Sermon on the Mount
Eberhard Arnold
Talks and writings on the transformative power of a life lived by Jesus' revolutionary teachings in the Sermon on the Mount.

Why We Live in Community
Eberhard Arnold and Thomas Merton
Foreword by Basil Pennington
In this time-honored manifesto, Arnold and Merton add their voices to the vital discussion of what real community is all about: love, joy, unity, and the great "adventure of faith" shared with others along the way.

Anni

Letters and Writings of Annemarie Wächter

Edited by Marianne Wright and Erna Albertz

In the swirl of 1920s Germany, a young woman comes of age.

No Lasting Home

A Year in the Paraguayan Wilderness

Emmy Barth

A sequel to *A Joyful Pilgrimage*. Tells the story of mothers, fathers and children escaping Hitler's persecution – their only refuge: the jungles of Paraguay. A gripping tale of faith tested by adversity.

Plough Publishing House

www.plough.com or info@plough.com

PO BOX 398, Walden, NY 12586, USA

Robertsbridge, East Sussex TN32 5DR, UK

4188 Gwydir Highway, Elsmore, NSW 2360, Australia

CPSIA information can be obtained
at www.ICGtesting.com
Printed in the USA
FFOW04n0353130218
45056946-45439FF

A Joyful Pilgrimage